Play Winning Golf

BEAT THE HAZARDS

Peter Smith

SACKVILLE
BOOKS

First published in 1990
by Sackville Books Ltd
Stradbroke Suffolk England

© Sackville Design Group Ltd
Text © Peter Smith
Illustrations © Ken Lewis

Designed and produced by Sackville Design Group Ltd
Art Director: Rolando Ugolini
Editor: Mike Henderson
Designer: Robert Yost

British Library Cataloguing in Publication Data
Smith, Peter
Beat the hazards. – (Play winning golf;2).
1. Golf. Techniques
I. Title II. Series

ISBN 0-948615-35-4

Typeset by Anglia Photoset Ltd, Colchester, Essex, England.

Reproduction by David Bruce Graphics, London, England
Printed and bound in Italy by New Interlitho SPA, Milan

Contents

Peter Smith

The author Peter Smith has worked as a writer and marketing consultant for over twenty-five years. He has published books on travel, classical composers and the painter Constable. Peter also paints, primarily in oils.

Widely travelled, he has worked as a journalist in the aviation and travel industries, and was the editor of travel magazines in London and New York. Peter lives in Madrid, Spain.

Introduction

In taking lessons around the world to help me beat the hazards, again and again the professionals have emphasized one golden rule; the best way to beat hazards is to avoid them. It sounds obvious, I know, but out on the course it is all too easy to forget this fundamental. Hazards are designed to penalise us so if we avoid them then we don't have to make recovery shots from difficult situations.

Unfortunately, all too often I must admit that my good intentions don't prevent me from making close acquaintances with every kind of hazard. Heavy rough, inpenetrable bushes, tall trees, deep water and steep-faced bunkers all seem to sometimes have an almost magical attraction for my ball. In this book I have been taught how best to deal with these situations, and a few more besides, like psychological hazards and playing in difficult weather conditions.

Another of the golden rules to emerge is not to rush shots if we do find ourselves in a difficult situation, but to take the time to think clearly what is the best way to deal with the problem. Rushed, intemperate shots in a hazard can easily lead to a quite unnecessary number of shots being dropped and scorecards ruined.

But of course dealing with hazards very much involves techniques and I am sure that in these pages you will find much advice that will help you to come to terms with, and finally to beat, the hazards.

Cannes–Mougins, France

Richard Sorrell, Assistant Professional

Bushes and trees

Not too far inland from the sophisticated Mediterranean resort of Cannes, on France's Côte D'Azur, is the famous Cannes–Mougins golf course, where, during the 1940s and 1950s, Henry Cotton was the head professional. The Cannes Open is held each spring on this beautiful course, set in the forests which lead up to the high mountains of the Alps-Maritimes. Past winners include Ballesteros, Norman, David Frost and Mark McNulty. The course record, a sizzling 64, eight under par, was set by Ian Woosnam in 1987.

Today the head professional is one of the leading exponents of teaching in France, Michel Damiano, a man who sees golf as a game to play in the mind. Michel's ideas on strategy are not so much revolutionary as pure common-sense. Assisting him are several younger professionals, all of whom are highly respected in their own right, and none more so than Englishman Richard Sorrell, who was invited here in late 1988, since when he has built up an enviable reputation for himself as a thorough and highly professional teacher.

I accompanied Richard one cold, wet morning as he gave a lesson to a small group of club members. Our little group tackled one of those difficult shots where the ball decides to run

Richard Sorrell, who came to Cannes-Mougins from England.

6

If you are close to a tree you must have a clear idea of what you want to do. Check that you can get the club face into the ball without hitting the tree.

and hide under a huge bush. Getting the ball out is daunting, to say the least.

"You need, of course, to be able to see the ball," Richard explained. "To do this you can push away any branches that are in your way, providing you don't break them off or stand on them to allow yourself a proper backswing."

Any idea of taking a chain-saw or mini combine harvester to rid your local course of troublesome trees and bushes is, I regret, not permitted under the rules of golf.

"I would suggest you play the ball off the front of your right foot, if you can get a comfortable position. Your backswing will, in all probability, be severely restricted so take a few practice backswings until you are happy with the position. This may, of course, restrict the length you can hit the ball and the direction it will go. What you are trying to do here is to recover from a very difficult situation so don't expect miracles.

"Try a 7-iron, with which most club golfers are happiest. As you are playing the ball back in your stance so much, with your hands well ahead of the ball, the effect will be to reduce the loft considerably, but you still want to have some loft coming into

the back of the ball. Anything more than a 7-or 6-iron will tend to give you a straight club face, with no loft.

"Grip right down on the club, again giving you more control. Then, depending on the room you have for the backswing, all you can do is to try to knock it out clear of the bushes."

If you are close to the green, say about 30 yards away, you might be able to run the ball onto the green if you can hit it hard enough – particularly if you have a down slope to work with.

Otherwise all you can hope for is to knock it to a position from which you can safely get near the flag on the next shot.

Of course, if you are 100 yards or so away from the green then all you can reasonably hope for is to hit the ball out to a safe spot for the next shot. Never risk staying in the bushes.

Ball under bushes. Grip well down with the wrists firm and club face hooded. Pull your arms and shoulders forward through the ball to generate power.

"This shot is really a stab at the ball," Richard explained to us. "Have the weight predominantly on the left side and stay still during the shot. Because the hands start so far forward they are in a locked position throughout the stroke, the wrists staying firm in the angle set at the address.

"The feeling on this shot is of pulling the hands through the ball, from right to left. The ball will stay low, not rising much off the ground, so if you have a bunker to cross you have a problem and should be looking for another area around the green to safely aim at.

"The other option, which you must consider if you have a really nasty situation, is to declare the ball unplayable. Lift it, take a penalty stroke and drop it in a clear area, within two club-lengths of the spot from where you lifted it but not nearer the hole. Make sure, though, that the area you have to drop in is safe and doesn't present you with a further set of problems."

Apart from bushes, trees can cause us endless problems, either getting in the way of the ball or blocking the view. With staked trees you can move the ball, but when the ball is behind a tree you need to be able to 'bend' it to get out of trouble. When the ball is resting up against the tree, though, quite another type of shot is needed.

"Here," said Richard, "your main concern is to get a clear takeaway from the ball, avoiding hitting the tree."

His suggested club was a 9-iron, because the aim is to get the club coming down into the back of the ball, so the club face is closed as it comes into contact. Using a sand-wedge would risk bouncing the club off the tree and topping or missing the ball.

"Address the ball with the *toe* of the club; this gives you more room on the backswing. A smooth takeaway and a fairly short backswing should help you come back into the ball at the right angle. But again the distance you can hope to achieve is limited if the ball is really right up against the tree trunk.

"Because of the difficulty of playing this shot it may be necessary to go in a different direction from your intended target. However, don't risk any of those amazing back-handed shots that you might have seen some Tour pros use."

Unless you are just playing a game for fun and don't mind taking eight those trick shots are purely for the video.

"This type of shot once again needs a fairly even stance, the weight being almost level depending on the terrain, and the body not moving much through the short swing. Grip down on the club for more control."

So, the one thing to remember on these shots, is that you are *escaping from a difficult situation*.

Don't expect to hit winners.

St Pierre, Gwent, UK

Renton Doig, Head Professional

Trees and using the driver

"This tree has stood here for over 350 years," Renton Doig, the head professional at the prestigious St Pierre Golf club in Chepstow, just across the Severn Bridge from England in Wales, told me in response to my question as to whether it was a stake-tree. Its magnificent nine-feet girth rather negated my claim for a free drop. It came as no surprise really but it was worth a try!

What did surprise me, however, was Renton's suggested club for getting out of this hazardous situation, the ball being ten yards behind the massive chestnut, under overhanging branches. The green, some 100 yards away, was totally obscured by the ancient tree. There are many fine chestnuts on this liberally tree-dotted course which hosts the Epson Grand Prix, a competition which until 1989 was played as a matchplay event but has since changed to strokeplay.

Obviously what was needed was a club that would keep the ball low, carry 100 yards, and fade. Well, what would you use?

Renton reached into my bag and took out the *driver*. Noting the obvious surprise on my face he explained why.

"For the distance you have left to the green, you would

Renton Doig, Head Professional at St Pierre. St Pierre hosts the Epson Grand Prix and the course has fine trees.

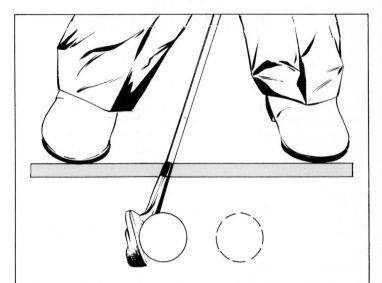

The ball position for aiming low with a long iron. Position the ball one club-head inside the right foot. This will help take the loft off the ball.

probably ideally need a 4- or 5-iron, but that would put the ball up in the air very quickly and you'd hit the overhanging branches, deflecting it who knows where.

"By using a driver you will keep the ball low, and impart enough left to right spin to get clear of the tree and get the ball somewhere near the green."

Renton explained that the straighter the face of the club the more slice spin you put on the ball, therefore a driver, with only 11° of loft against a pitching wedge with 50°, will move the ball with much more slice. That is why many golfers complain they slice their woods yet are able to hit irons straighter.

With the club selected and a reasonable understanding of what was likely to happen to the ball and why, it was down to the practicalities of the shot. Renton took me through the pre-shot details.

"First, your grip. This should be the same as your normal correct grip. Secondly, your aim. Align the club so that the club face points to where you want the ball to finish" – in this case on the green so the aiming point was, in fact, straight through the tree.

"You need to have the ball off your left heel, as for a normal drive, and your feet, hips and shoulders aligned left, approximately 20° left of the ball-to-target line.

The target of the ball is straight ahead but feet, hips and shoulders aim left to get slice on the ball.

"Be sure to stand up fairly straight," Renton told me, "don't slouch over the ball."

The first attempt – I think my first ever in using a driver off the fairway – ended in abject failure. I failed to swing through completely, holding back on the shot, subsequently topping it – yet still sending it about sixty yards and beginning to fade it, leaving me with a fairly easy pitch in for the third shot and a hopeful bogey-five.

That was enough, in retrospect, to achieve the first object of any hazardous shot – get the ball back in play without doing too much damage.

For the next attempt Renton made sure I was concentrating oh swinging through the ball, not trying to hit it as most golfers do. "Always swing *through* the ball, not at it!" he suggested.

"Never play a wood off the back foot, always just inside the front heel," he emphasized. "Treat the shot exactly as you would off a tee, though obviously you need to hit the ball on its centre, not slightly underneath."

The next attempt, with a full follow-through, was more successful, keeping the ball low under the branches of the tree, fading it and hitting it to the green. If anything I slightly over-hit for the ball ended right of the green in light rough but pin high. This left an easy chip and run to a couple of feet from the flag.

"Do make sure you are far enough behind the tree to use fade, though," warned Renton. "Any less than about fifteen yards makes it difficult, depending on the amount of fade you want.

"And make sure you finish with a full follow-through!"

We moved on a few holes to the sixteenth to do battle with another of St Pierre's magnificent trees.

The hole dog-legs right with trees on both sides. Many players slice their tee-shot into the trees on the right. The difficulties here are getting a line to the green (which is, realistically, out of reach) and keeping the ball low enough to avoid the overhanging branches, some of which come down to only four feet off the ground.

"This requires a long iron with loft taken off," Renton advised. "Take a 3- or 4-iron, position the ball one club-head inside the right foot, and slightly hood the face. Don't close it, turning the toe slightly inwards, but 'hood' it, turning the top of the club face over slightly, while keeping the face square to the target.

"Take a couple of practice backswings, particularly if you are under trees, because you want to make sure that no branches interfere with the swing. Remember that the actual swing will be longer than any practice swings. Also be sure to take those practice swings right above the ball, not six inches away – that could make all the difference.

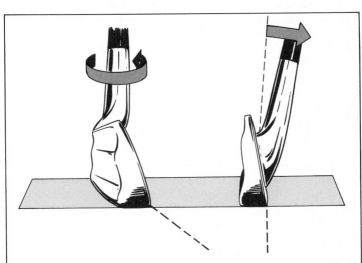

(Left) Closing the face by turning the toe slightly inwards to hit the ball left of your body line. (Right) Hooding the face by turning the top of the face over slightly to reduce loft but keeping it square to the target.

The club on the ground indicates the normal ball position but to keep the ball low Renton Doig has it back in his stance.

"In a case like this where you want the ball low and straight, having decided a line through the trees to a suitable spot on the fairway, you have to use a punchier shot, with a three-quarter backswing and only about a half follow-through. Keep your wrists firm. Don't turn them over as you would for a normal shot but end with the back of the left hand still facing upwards.

"Also, as you are trying to keep the ball low you need to keep your weight more on the left side. When you're in a position where you need to get the ball up quickly you lean back on the right leg, sweeping under the ball. Here it's the opposite so the weight is on the left leg. As you hit down you pull the ball forward."

We experimented a couple of times before getting it right, then moved on to our final challenge, a situation where we wanted to pull the ball right to left round a tree, drawing it rather than fading.

"Here," Renton told me, "the thing you must do is close the face of the club, turning the toe inwards until the face aims at the exact target, which happens to be directly behind the tree. Therefore you aim the clubface at the tree, and stand with your shoulder, hips and feetline to the right of the tree. Remember that the ball has to start right of the tree and be drawn round it to the left.

"With all of these shots," Renton concluded, "you will need practice to get the position and techniques correct. But they are well worth the effort as they can save you several strokes out on the golf course."

Bay Hill, Florida, USA
Allen Self, Head Professional

Playing on Bermuda grass

Florida is becoming ever more popular as a golf vacation destination. The Sunshine State has always been popular with Americans but it is now attracting Europeans, too. However, one thing about golf in Florida that is different from many other parts of the world, including most of Europe – apart from the welcome winter sunshine – is the grass. It looks different, feels different and, requires a different type of shot.

"You can spin and control shots far easier on this type of grass," Allen Self the Head Golf Professional at the sumptuous Bay Hill Club just outside Orlando, told me as we walked out on the course one glorious November afternoon with the temperature over 30°C (86 °F).

"On the grass here in Florida you have to hit the ball with a firmly descending blow into the back of the ball, following

"Don't replace divots on Bermuda grass" warns Allen Self, the Head Professional at Bay Hill, Florida.

With a steep lie like this on a bunker lip, put all the weight on the left leg. Grip right down the shaft. The clubhead should hit the grass almost horizontally.

through to take a divot well after the ball. This angle of attack gets that ball high fast, and allows you to control both the spin of the ball and its length.

"With grass in Europe, and some other parts of the United States, several blades will get between the clubface and ball, so you never get a totally 'true' shot. Here, there is no grass between the face and ball, just direct club/ball contact. That allows better control.

"To hit the ball this way you need to have it back in your stance further than normal, with your weight slightly more left.

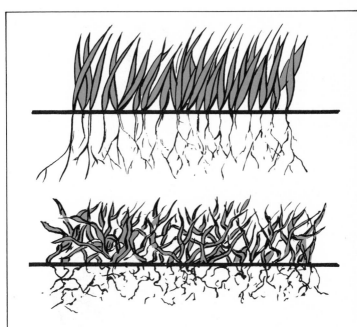

(Above) Bent grass traditionally used in northern climates.
(Below) Bermuda grass, from hotter climates, grows across
and not upwards like bent grass. Bermuda grass is less
forgiving to play on than traditional grasses.

That will help to promote that steep downward hit.''

This *Bermuda* grass only grows in hot weather and can be killed off quite easily by temperatures below about 3°C. It is far less forgiving than other grasses, so a miss hit shot is likely to end up anywhere, normally well short of the target.

Sure enough, as I tried it, I topped a couple before finding the right spot to hit. You do have to be far more precise than on other grass. The couple I did connect properly with, using a 9-iron, flew high and straight at the flag, 120 yards away, coming down on the green and stopping almost immediately, with very little run. The divot began about an inch further on from where the ball had been.

Remembering those constant exhortations to 'replace your divot', I moved forward scooping up handfuls of strands of grass before Allen stopped me.

''Replacing divots here will destroy the course,'' he told me before going on to explain. ''Bermuda grass grows *across*, not upwards like bent grass, which is most common on European

On Bermuda grass the ball sits up more, so you need to hit the ball before the ground, hitting down into the back of it. This gets it airborne more quickly and the backspin helps it 'sit-down' well on landing.

and more northern American courses. On those types of grass you would replace the divot so that it would start to root again and grow properly. With Bermuda grass, all that would happen is that a replaced divot would hinder the cross growth of new grass, and you would end up with a brown patch that would eventually sink, leaving an indentation in the fairway.''

We subsequently found a few tell-tale patches where unknowing players had replaced their divots. ''All golf carts in

Florida carry special little pots of a sand and peat mixture. Just fill in the divot, tap it down firmly and it will help the cross growth of the grass.

"But don't be scared of hitting the grass and taking a divot – on this surface it's very difficult to take it cleanly off the surface because, as it is so springy, the club will just bounce off and you'll top it."

The top pros actually prefer this type of surface for it gives them greater control over the length of the shot, but then they hit almost perfect shots every time. Many Tour pros live in Florida, several of them on the Bay Hill course.

Just off the 18th green is the splendid home of Scott Hoch; Payne Stewart has a house on the 12th; 'Tommy' Nakajima on the 10th; Nick Price lives just down the road; and the legendary Arnold Palmer lives on the marina just a short 5-wood from the club-house. Mr Palmer's office is right above the club-house. The Arnold Palmer Golf Academy, for America's best golfing youngsters, was based here when Allen Self first arrived in 1984. The course is a composite of three nines, with the championship course for the annual Nestlé Invitational (formerly the Bay Hill Classic) comprising the Challenger and Champion courses. The final hole is rated the most difficult on the US Tour.

One further problem encountered by visiting golfers is the thicker grass which they call 'the rough', particularly lining the outside banks of bunkers. Again, because it grows across, it almost gobbles the ball up, often making it difficult to see.

"In cases like this," Allen told me, "you need to treat it like a bunker shot, hitting a couple of inches behind the ball. Position the ball in the back of your stance and keep your weight on the left side, drawing the club down into the grass behind the ball.

"As you hit into that grass, it will lift the ball up, like sand, pop it up high, and make it sit down as it lands on the green."

Sure enough, as I hit behind it, the ball popped up almost vertically, leaving the club in the ground (there's nowhere for it to go); on landing it just sat still.

"So you must go for the pin," Allen emphasized. "The length of the backswing determines the distance you'll achieve, but you are limited."

On a flat surface in that 'rough' you need to adopt a similar position, ball right, weight left and punch down behind the ball. That will give you more distance, yet still help you to keep control.

A last word from Allen, "On the fairway, don't be scared of hitting the grass and taking a huge divot after you've hit the ball. In this climate the grass will grow back quite quickly."

Poniente, Mallorca
Brian Salter, Club Professional

Playing on hard fairways

The Balearic Islands, set in the shimmering blue of the Mediterranean enjoy long, serene periods of sunshine. The island of Mallorca is by far the biggest of the group and, besides its famous golden beaches, has remote forests and secluded bays, particularly on the northern coast. Less well known, however, are its excellent and testing golf courses.

Not far from the capital, Palma de Mallorca, is Poniente Golf Club – eighteen varied holes with every conceivable hazard thrown in – lakes, trees, bunkers, uphill shots, downhill shots and just plain difficult ones. The course, though fascinating to play, requires careful thought and a bagful of different shots.

Peter Smith and Brian Salter on a hard fairway at Poniente. It pays to be able to cope with these surfaces.

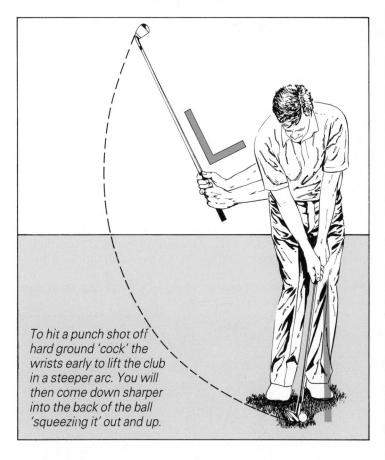

To hit a punch shot off hard ground 'cock' the wrists early to lift the club in a steeper arc. You will then come down sharper into the back of the ball 'squeezing it' out and up.

The professional at the club is Englishman Brian Salter.

The Mallorcan sunshine has its effect on the golf course, baking the fairways hard in the hot summer months. Playing shots off hard fairways – or off paths and other hard surfaces – demands a different type of shot. Many of us, unaccustomed to playing off such surfaces, end up topping the ball.

"Quite simply," says Brian Salter, "the club just bounces off the hard surface and fails to make proper contact with the ball.

"The best club to use is a fairway wood, because you need to have a long, low, sweeping motion through the ball.

"With an iron the club will bounce more and probably hit the top of the ball, only sending it a couple of dozen yards. The wood, either a 3 or a 5, will get more body behind the ball. And, because it is played more like a drive, with the ball forward of the centre of the stance, almost off the left instep, the club will

A good exercise to 'cock' the wrists early. Set the wrists with the club horizontal before attempting to swing. This keeps the hands in the right position.

hit it slightly on the up-stroke. That in turn gives more distance.''

One thing that is impossible on hard fairways is taking a divot – the ground is too hard to dig into. The use of a wood, with that sweeping motion, takes the ball cleanly off the fairway and so does not take a divot anyway.

''Even the player who slightly tops the ball with a fairway wood will still achieve reasonable distance, for the club head gets behind the ball and powers it forward, putting topspin on it which will make the ball run and run.

''For the higher handicapper, using an iron off a hard, close fairway for a long shot could be suicidal,'' Brian continued.

Moving closer in towards the green, in the 50–90 yard range, Brian still suggested a wood, either a 5 or a 7 if you have one.

''This, though, depends on whether you have a direct line into the green. Vary the length of the swing according to the distance you need, but still play the ball off the inside of the left foot – forward in the stance. A 5-wood will get the ball airborne and, with the soft greens on this course, the ball will sit down nicely when it lands."

Brian explained that the 5-wood is also useful when you have a narrow aiming point, as on the approach to the 4th green at Poniente, which is guarded by trees on either side.

"There, the 5-wood, with a half or three-quarter backswing, will help maintain control over the direction but will still give better distance than might an iron."

Moving in very close to the green we came to a position no more than 50 yards from the pin but with a hazard in the way. A wood here would over-hit the shot. This, Brian explained, needed something totally different.

"Whatever you do, don't use a sand wedge on a hard fairway – or a track or path. The sand wedge has a sole that comes into the ground first before the club face hits the ball. It would just bounce off the surface and miss the ball completely, or hit it so thin that the ball would just trickle forward.

"A club with high loft but with the club face as the leading edge, is needed. The pitching wedge is made for this.

"Position the ball slightly back of centre of the stance, the hands just pressing forward a little, but not too much (otherwise you end up with no loft on the club). The wrists are slightly cocked and held firm through the swing. Swing fairly steeply into the back of the ball. The idea is to play a little punch shot, the club face coming down into the back of the ball, putting backspin on it. That gets the ball airborne to carry the hazard, and makes it stop on landing. The punch shot will, however, keep the ball lower than normal, but if you hit it right you will still get the right amount of backspin.

"Try to continue the follow-through, though; don't just hit and stop the club dead. To do that you need to turn the body to the target as you would with a fuller shot, though the weight transfer has to be at the very last moment. On a full shot the weight transfer begins at the top of the backswing, the body turning through the ball to power the shot. On this shot, though, the half backswing takes place with the body held stable. As you come down into the back of the ball, 'nipping' it, the weight transfer takes place onto the left side. You must, however, start with the weight about 60 per cent on the left side.

"That weight transfer is perhaps the most critical part of this shot, and must be practised," Brian emphasized.

"The other major point to remember on a short, punch shot like this is to avoid closing the club face. Because the hands are

The follow-through off hard ground. The club face should be pointing straight out, not up or down. It must be square to the target. Swing through to the horizontal position.

slightly ahead of the ball you 'hood' the club face, fractionally turning it more over the ball. However, you must avoid turning the toe in, round the ball. That will just hook it left. Make sure that the club face is square to the target. Try standing with a slightly open stance to the target rather than square. That will help you to get the maximum loft out of the shot.''

Hitting shots such as these is not easy, and they are not needed every week, because in countries such as the United Kingdom most people have the opportunity to play off fairly lush fairways. Yet from time to time, when the ground is exceptionally hard, or you have landed on a path or cart-track, it is vital to know how to play this particular type of shot. Brian's advice, to use either a wood off the fairway or, closer in, to hit a low, 'punch' shot, could save you wasting a shot or two. And what a difference that can make to your round!

Portmarnock,
Republic of Ireland
Assistant Professional: Colin Cassidy

Rough

In every round of golf I play – and I suspect you're the same – the ball always ends up, at some stage, in places other than on the fairway! bunkers, trees, the odd lake, gorse bushes are all regular visiting spots. I do like variety!

I now have less fear of bunkers, having spent several hours practising scooping balls out of the Hell Bunker at St Andrews. Trees, too, are less of a menace these days, yet one hazard that always gives me a problem is rough. And my ball, in every round, decides to dig itself deep into this horrible stuff!

To find out how to play safely out of this dreaded situation I went along to Portmarnock Golf Club a dozen miles north of Dublin's fair city where, as the rhyme goes, 'the girls are so pretty'. Which is something which can not be said for some of the positions Colin Cassidy, Assistant Pro at Portmarnock, discovered for us as.

"For really thick rough you have to play a special type of shot," Colin told me, dropping the ball in a mass of green.

The ball was just visible and, as Colin explained, the only

Portmarnock, surrounded by the sea on three sides, is a superb links course. The view is across the eighth green.

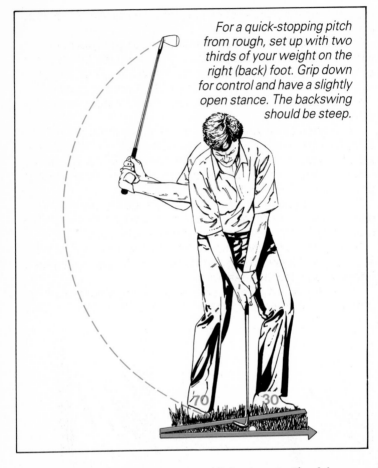

For a quick-stopping pitch from rough, set up with two thirds of your weight on the right (back) foot. Grip down for control and have a slightly open stance. The backswing should be steep.

possibility was to attempt to get it back onto the fairway.

The first thing to do was to walk onto the fairway to have a look at where the next shot, ideally, could be taken from with the approach to the green being better from the right side of the fairway it was obvious that the further out we could get the ball from its position on the left, the better.

"Put all your weight on the right foot," said Colin. "Take a very open stance as you would for a bunker shot, with the club face sitting nearly horizontal."

He suggested a sand wedge for this, or a really flat wedge if you have one.

"The aim is to slide the club under the ball, as you would in a bunker, scooping it out as high as possible. As in a bunker shot don't ground the club first – it might dislodge the ball in which case you incur a penalty shot – and aim one centimetre behind the ball."

I tried this a few times before managing to get it out high and, although not in a perfect position, at least on the fairway. The difference between success and failure was very fine, but Colin showed me, quite simply, why some attempts came good.

"The follow-through." he said and demonstrated the difference to me.

"If you don't turn your body in a full follow through, with the body facing the target, you'll fail to lift the ball out." Once again a club pro was teaching me something so basic, yet something which makes so much difference. It really is the little things in golf which make the difference.

"Although you should have an aiming point, never attempt to go for too much distance on a shot in really heavy rough," he reiterated, "just concentrate on getting the ball out."

Having mastered this – no doubt I shall still hit bad ones, but at least now I know what I should be doing! – we moved on to lighter rough, just off the fairway.

"Here you stand a better chance of having a fairly good lie, particularly if the grass is growing towards the hole," Colin

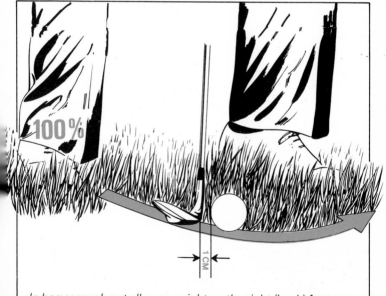

In heavy rough put all your weight on the right (back) foot. Take a very open stance as you would for a bunker shot, with the club-face sitting nearly horizontal.

pointed out. "If it's against you, you have a problem and you should again scoop it out with a wedge.

"If the lie is good though, go down a club, taking an eight instead of a seven, for example, and close the face slightly. With grass between the club face and the ball you're likely to get a 'flier', so grip down very slightly and feel that you have better control."

This set-up helps to keep the ball lower and can be used when you want a reasonable distance but don't have any obstacles to get over, like a bunker or trees.

Moving on to the green we found a wonderful piece of rough about 45 yards from the pin, with a bunker in between. The green, the eighth on the nine-hole 'C' course at Portmarnock, is tiny, just 35 yards from to back and about 15 across, with a bunker at either side. It is also two-tier and has bushes just off to the left, from the tee. We took the ball off the fairway into the rough on the right, leaving a pitch of 40 yards to clear the bunker, but then only 15 yards for it to stop before running off the other side, either into the bunker or the bushes. The pin was seven yards from the right side of the green. The type of shot we all love!

Colin demonstrated just how simple it was to get out and land the ball on the green. He just gripped down on a sand wedge, swung steeply and slowly and finished high. The ball responded. But when I tried, it was not with the same success.

"This is the type of shot where 'feel' is vital," Colin explained.

"The weight is still on the right side, but not like before. Here it is probably 70/30 on the right. Use a sand wedge, grip down

In light rough if the grass is growing against you, close the club-face slightly.

28

for control, open the face as for a bunker shot, and swing on the path of the feet, bringing the club out-to-in. This slides the club face under the ball, 'cutting' it up into the air high.''
' ''It's vital, though, that the club really be pulled through the ball, more with the shoulders from the back because the backswing is more upright than for a normal shot. Yet it must be slow. Very slow, otherwise you just snatch at the ball.''

He demonstrated and had me practising until I was getting the ball out high. The answer is in the follow through, and the way the club is pulled through. The speed determines the distance, but it is vital to finish fully turned to the target – that means the target as the line of the feet, not the pin, because the stance and club face are open. The finishing position had me facing back to the tee!

This is one area of the game where practise to get the right feel is vital, but the essentials have to be understood and adhered to if you are to be successful. Colin repeated them.

''Weight more on the right.
''Club-face and stance very open.
''Grip down.
''A steep backswing.
''Slow, slow swing.
''Pull the club through the ball.
''Full follow-through.''

If the grass is growing towards the hole, open the club face a little. Checking the direction that the grass grows in is a good habit to get into.

Wörthsee, Germany
Jonathan Mills, Club Professional

Beating water hazards

Most people have heard of the so-called Bermuda Triangle which is an area in the Atlantic off the coast of the southern United States. It is infamous for the apparently inexplicable disappearance of ships and aircraft without trace.

It came, therefore, as something of a surprise to find another 'Bermuda Triangle' in the Bavarian forests not too far away from Munich. This is infamous too, for the loss of golf balls without trace – but there the similarity ends for their disappearance can be explained quite simply.

"The swing!" said Jonathan Mills, the head professional at Wörthsee, home since 1989 of the Lufthansa Ladies' German Open championship. The 'Triangle' comprises three holes on the turn, where water plays a major part and a score card can so easily be ruined by recklessness.

Holes ten, eleven and twelve form a triangle with water and out-of-bounds coming heavily into play on all three, particularly the short and very difficult eleventh with its two lakes.

The entire area is hazardous and a good test of the best strategy of conquering hazards – *by avoiding them*!

"That really is so much better than having to attempt difficult shots from positions that, for the average club golfer, are almost impossible. He would be better advised to play more controlled shots with an iron than trying to hit long woods and spraying them all over the place," said Jonathan.

The first hole in the 'triangle' is a good example. The fairway itself is only 45 yards across at the widest point but, unusually, has out-of-bounds on either side, with water hazards down the left and across the fairway in front of the green.

"The aiming point is slightly left of centre and not too long," said Jonathan.

Far from using a driver he suggested a 4-iron off the tee, and showed me a very easy way of ensuring that the ball is teed at

The 'Bermuda Triangle' of three holes on the turn surrounded by water at Wörthsee. Out-of-bounds comes heavily into play. The key is to know how to avoid the hazards.

the right height for this type of shot. This is often a problem for club golfers who want to hit a good iron shot. For woods, most people suggest that the top of the club should be on the equator of the ball. For the irons the majority of players tend to tee it too low.

"Place the tee between two fingers and just push it in with the thumb," demonstrated Jonathan.

The water across the fairway comes into play at about 200 yards off the tee and finishes about 65 yards short of the green. The best shot, therefore, is a 4-iron of about 160–170 yards, allowing the second shot to be aimed at the left side of the green, completely skirting the danger of the lake.

"So many players, particularly if they have hit a pretty good tee-shot, are tempted to have a go at the green with the second.

"However, that is flirting with danger for the green is protected by bunkers on either side and has out of bounds at

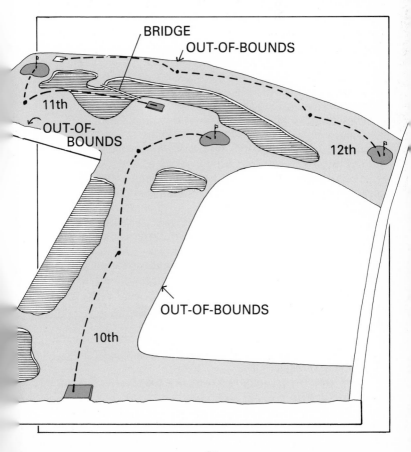

Jonathan Mills, the Club Professional at Wörthsee.

the back. The best shot if you have hit 160–170 yards off the tee is a gentle 7-iron to the left 'safe' side of the green from where a little bump-and-run shot will have you on the green in three.

"Keep the ball low on these close approach shots if you can," recommended Jonathan. "You have more control over shots that stay low.

"*The art of playing hazard shots is knowing how to avoid them*," he re-stated, telling me something that is so simple and basic that most of us always forget it.

The 11th is a real 'killer' of a hole, 177 yards across two lakes, with the ladies' tee and a dropping area on an island lying in between them.

"This is where so many people ruin their entire round," Jonathan told me, mentioning that quite a few professionals drop strokes here as well. "Most amateurs become scared of the water and either over-club, using a 3-wood, or they use a long iron and lose control."

Either way the penalty is severe – a lost ball and a penalty stroke.

We stood quietly aside and watched three groups of players come through. Of seven players, five hit the water, one went out-of-bounds on the left and only one hit the green. Most of those in the water used a 3-wood.

"On the last hole I suggest a 4-iron to hit 160–170 yards," said Jonathan, "but here many players, because it's a long par-3, think they should take a driver. Yet we have 177 yards to go so a 4-iron would be ideal again if they could hit it straight. The best shot would be to go to the left of the green, using a 7-iron which is more controllable for the average golfer, and then pitch to the green safely, without having to worry about the lake. Take the hazard out of the game!

"Line it up properly, aim slightly left, as most club golfers slice, and swing smoothly. Play sensible golf."

"What happens if you do land in the water?" I asked.

"Two choices," he told me. "Either take another off the tee, adding a penalty stroke, or walk forward to this hole's dropping area and hit a second ball, again adding the penalty stroke."

The sensible thing, of course, is to walk forward the 75 yards to the dropping zone and leave yourself with 100 yards to go to the flag.

"You often see someone put the first ball into the water with, say, a 3-wood, then tee the next ball up and hit the same club!" said Jonathan. "Why make the same mistake twice? If the 3-wood has put the ball in the water the first time, the chances are that it will do it the second!

"You took the chance with the first shot – play safe!"

We moved on to the 12th, a 400 yard par five with an index of 18, so most players need to make it in five. The first shot, again

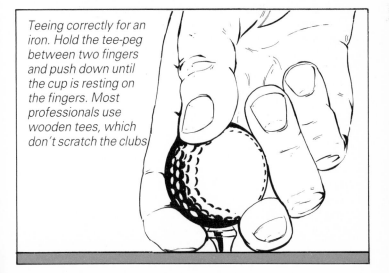

Teeing correctly for an iron. Hold the tee-peg between two fingers and push down until the cup is resting on the fingers. Most professionals use wooden tees, which don't scratch the clubs.

Getting distance on your shots. As the club comes into the back of the ball 'walk through' the shot as you would with a drive in tennis. Drive the shot with the knees and feet. The left knee comes round to be, like the body, facing the target in a well-balanced finish.

carrying the same lake, is to a narrow landing area with out-of-bounds to the left (the main highway into Munich) and a hazard to the right (dry when I visited it but classified as a water hazard so you can't ground your club in it). The 4-iron was the best bet here, too.

The second shot is, perhaps, easier but requires more distance if you are to attack the green. However, for the club golfer getting distance is a problem. Or is it?

"Improving your distance is all in the swing," explained Jonathan. "Too many golfers, particularly high-handicap players, tend to swing from the top downwards. The good golfer swings from the ground up."

He demonstrated how a golfer should 'walk through the ball,' using the knees and hips to 'drive' through the ball.

"Tennis is the perfect analogy. When you hit a good forehand you are turning your whole body into the ball, not standing totally still and just thrashing your arm at it. It's the same in golf. Kick into the ball, knees and hips pulling the body round to the hitting position.

"I don't necessarily go along with the straight left arm at address position, either," he continued. "The body needs to be relaxed, not tense. Although golf is not as physically demanding as some other sports, you still need to be supple and athletic. You must feel relaxed and comfortable."

The approach shot to this green ended in light rough to the right, giving Jonathan the opportunity to demonstrate a recovery shot from this type of 'hazard'.

"It really is dependent on the lie of the ball," he said as we walked to the ball. "If it is sitting up on fluffy, long grass lying in the direction of the hole you will be able to play it out with a 6- or 7-iron, depending on the distance.

"Be careful not to ground the club near the ball if it is sitting up," he warned me. "This could move the ball and incur a penalty stroke. I always suggest that you open the club a little, and take one club extra. The reason is that long grass will tend to close the club face at impact, which is why, in longer grass, many high-handicap golfers tend to dig the ball in deeper.

"Measure the club to the bottom of the ball, not the ground, and adopt a slightly open stance. That, with the extra club, will give you the distance you need and knock the ball out safely from a position like this not too far from the green."

On the way back to the clubhouse, which was once a farmhouse in the days when the course was a series of maize-fields, we discussed equipment for the average golfer.

"Shots can be improved quite substantially by using the right equipment," Jonathan explained. "Today's clubs are an enormous improvement on the old ones. Their perimeter is weighted to bring the club face back to square at impact. Graphite shafts will also help as they are snappier and lighter – they really do make a difference."

While Jonathan, like most professionals, has a contract with a club manufacturer, I use graphite-shaft clubs which have demonstrably improved my striking ability, with extra weight in the head rather than in the shaft.

"Metal woods, too," Jonathan continued, "make a big difference, giving much better distance off the tee, by 10–20 yards on a well-struck shot. "Yet distance is only important if you plan where to put the ball!"

Commonwealth G.C., Melbourne, Australia

Phil O'Bryan, Teaching Professional

Bunkers

"An almost impossible situation to get out of in less than three," was how Phil O'Bryan, the assistant professional at the splendid Commonwealth Golf Club, a few miles south of Melbourne, described the situation I got myself into playing the short 9th.

A slightly pulled tee-shot sent the ball into the trees to the left of the green, behind a deep bunker which protects that side of it. To add to the difficulty the ball was under a tree with overhanging leaves and branches and so it could not be lofted high to clear the bunker and land softly, safely on the green. Apart from being rock-hard, the green slopes in a few places, giving an unpredictable bounce; the pin was just eight feet in from the edge of the bunker. The distance from the ball to the bunker was 18 yards.

"You could never expect to get up and down in two from here," Phil pronounced as we stood glumly surveying the scene from under the shade of the trees. "The only thing you can do is *to work out a strategy for getting a comfortable three*, rather than risking a damaging four from here, which would turn your score on this par-3 into a nasty five.

"What you must do is to play the shot that has the least risk attached to it, rather than a shot that would be spectacular if it works but has chances of 100–1 against.

"Getting to within fifteen feet of the pin from here is over

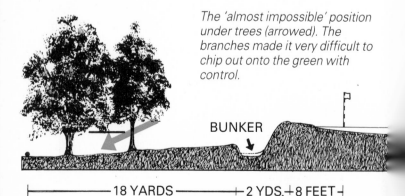

The 'almost impossible' position under trees (arrowed). The branches made it very difficult to chip out onto the green with control.

BUNKER

|———— 18 YARDS ————|— 2 YDS.—|—8 FEET—|

Phil O'Bryan of the Commonwealth GC recommends taking the time to work out a clear strategy in difficult situations.

100–1 against, and even that wouldn't guarantee a two, so really you have to admit that you will take three and then work out the easiest way of getting down in three shots."

The lie of the ball was good, sitting up nicely and with no overhanging branches behind the ball to restrict the backswing.

"If you do go over the bunker directly at the flag the ball will bounce and roll on 30–40 yards. The back of the green is out-of-bounds so you don't want to risk going too far."

We walked from the ball forwards to the bunker, pacing the distance, and then looked carefully at the bunker.

"Is it well raked? Is it hard? Is it full of water? These are the sort of questions," Phil continued, "to which you need answers. One of your options, if you are a good bunker player, would be to knock the ball into the bunker to a position from where you can be confident of hitting out close to the pin."

This particular bunker was relatively deep with a steep face, so that option could be ruled out here.

"What is the grassy bank above the face like?" Phil asked as we skirted around it to investigate the green.

OUT-OF-BOUNDS

"Is it soft and springy? Is it very steep? Could we hit the ball low to lodge on this bank or even bounce off it, taking pace off the ball as it just pops off the top of the bank?"

Again, this option had to be discounted. The bank was too steep and any ball hit at it would just roll down into the bunker. I know – we tried it!

On the green we looked at possible landing sites for the ball, taking time to visualize what could happen to the ball as it bounced on various spots.

Moving back to the ball Phil bent down, getting his eyes as close to it as possible – without laying flat on the ground, of course, which would be taking matters a bit too far.

"Try to really see the line the ball will take," he advised. "Look carefully at the overhanging foliage. Is it just leaves, which you could hit through, or are there any branches?

"Check the angle the ball will take by standing on the face of your club next to the ball. The shaft will give you the angle.

"More than anything else though, *take your time*! A professional could take a couple of minutes on this shot,

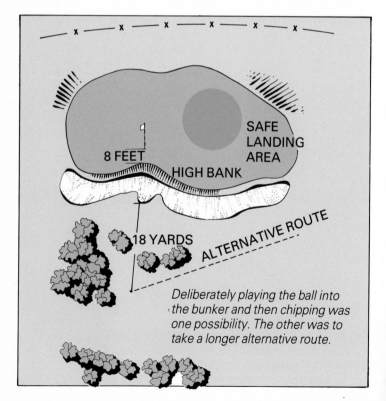

Deliberately playing the ball into the bunker and then chipping was one possibility. The other was to take a longer alternative route.

Take a minute to walk forward and look at where you might land the ball. Look at the green, the depth of the bunker, angle of the ridge, and think your way through the possibilities.

weighing up all the options, going through every possible shot in his mind. Most club players, by contrast, would just try to get out as quickly as possible, with little thought given to what type of shot they should play. They seem to be embarrassed by being in a hazardous situation and won't take the time to think their way out of it.

"I know slow play is the bane of golf, but when you're in a tricky situation you ought to take some time to think it through. There are plenty of other ways you can avoid wasting time on a golf course. Don't play slow golf – but never rush a shot!

"If you decide to go for the green you have to have worked out which side of the green presents you with the biggest target. In this case, it is the right-hand side of the green.

"Because the leaves on our angle are fairly thin, we can afford to go through the bottom of them. This will help take pace off the ball, but will also reduce spin, causing us to lose control on landing.

"Position the ball off the inside of the back foot, weight seventy per cent left and grip down on the club for control.

"You must hit the ball first, coming down into the back of the ball to give it backspin.

"The weight of the shot is vital and you should have a few

practice swings until you are comfortable. Don't feel rushed!

"The swing is all in the arms and shoulders, with very little body movement until after you have hit the ball. Then, be sure in your mind that you have chosen the right option. Know what the ball will do.

"The art of golf is knowing what shot to hit, when. Never try a shot you've never hit before, and don't try something you think you might be able to do. Even a shot like this little chip of 30 yards, you have hit many times before. The only difference today is that you have all these hazards in your mind. Blot them out – just hit a 30-yard chip!"

Using a pitching wedge, we did just that. Of six balls, one hit the bank and dropped into the bunker, one rolled off the green but not out-of-bounds, and four landed on the back right of the green, offering two putts for the four. With the stroke index that was good enough for a net par.

The other option, of course, was to chip out sideways onto the fairway, for a chip-and-run in to the pin, once again taking the time to walk out and thoroughly investigate the best possible landing.

Also look at the height that your club will put on the ball. Stand on the face – the shaft will give you the angle at which the ball will rise. Will this be too great? Will the ball hit the tree?

Hilversum, Holland
Martin Morbey, Club Professional

Getting out of the rough

The trouble with many of the golf books that I have read, written mostly by professional golfers, is that they frequently tell you how to hit perfect shots from perfect fairway positions every time. Now you and I know that we do not hit perfect shots every time, nor do we have perfect lies like those on the professional Tour courses.

More often than not the ball is nowhere *near* the fairway but in that patch of semi-jungle on either side of the fairway that the greenkeeper forgot to cut! Rough by name, and rough by nature too.

To varying degrees it is there on every hole and my round normally entails a half dozen or more visits to it. Getting out of it, without infuriatingly pushing it just a few yards to be confronted with the same shot again was the problem I took to Martin Morbey. Martin is the very popular golf professional at the Hilversumsche Golf Club near Hilversum, arguably the best club in Holland. Its membership list includes some of the elite of Dutch society.

Martin Morbey, Club Professional at Hilversum.

"When you're in the rough, your only priority is to get out," Martin told me on a rainy October morning. "Too many players, having watched the Tour pros hit marvellous recovery shots 200 yards out of the rough to an inch from the pin, believe they can do the same."

The problem with this, of course, is that the pros have far more talent – and the rough on Tour courses is often no worse than a poor municipal fairway. Add to that the fact that the pros do not usually go quite so far off the fairway, and you can see that it is a totally different game.

Martin's advice, echoed by golf professionals across the world, is to *go for position on the fairway for the next shot, forgetting distance*.

"Go for elevation – take the shortest route back to the safety of the fairway where you can see the green and get in a good next shot.

"You also find that, with golf course design, the shot from the rough will have another hazard in the way, as bunkers tend to be on the sides of greens rather than directly in front.

"If anything else is in the way, unless you are very close to the green and can be 100 per cent certain to get across, don't

The punch shot out of the rough. Be sure not to 'quit' on the shot. Keep your hands slightly in front of the ball and address the ball with the club off the ground.

When playing out of the rough with a lofted club use a fairly steep backswing and come down firmly onto the back of the ball, putting loft onto it immediately.

even attempt it. Get the ball to an area where your next shot will be hazard-free."

Avoiding hazards is, after all, better than playing out of them! Martin's next suggestion was to take your best friends into the rough with you. This idea rather stunned me until he explained: "In the rough your best friends are often your most lofted clubs.

"Using a lofted club, keeping the ball inside your right foot with your weight leaning left, use a fairly steep backswing so that you come onto the back of the ball firmly, putting loft on it immediately, getting it airborne and clear of trouble.

"It's also important to stand square to where you want the ball to go. Too many people stand too open and thus come across the ball, causing a weak rather than a strong shot." Martin also suggested aiming at the back of the ball, not behind.

The backswing and the follow-through need to be full. 'Quitting' on the shot will probably leave it still embedded in rough. It is the speed of the swing and not always the length, that dictates distance.

"Finish the club up on the left shoulder for every shot," he told me, "except for those little chips round the green."

For light rough – the sort that the pros occasionally have to play out of – the options are increased.

"If the ball is sitting up on a cushion of grass you might even be able to get a 5-wood at it. If the grass is growing towards the hole the large head of the wood will part the grass, beating a path to the ball as it were."

However, he stressed that the ball really needs to be hit on its centre and not underneath.

"Sweep it off the grass," he motioned. "Address the ball with the club off the ground too, so that you don't risk dislodging it

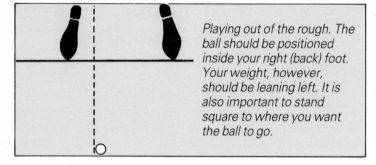

Playing out of the rough. The ball should be positioned inside your right (back) foot. Your weight, however, should be leaning left. It is also important to stand square to where you want the ball to go.

and incurring a penalty stroke. Keep your hands slightly in front of the ball and don't try anything fancy.

Many average players, I suggested, are scared of hitting a flier out of longer grass and thus hold back on the shot.

"Be honest. How many times do you hit a ball past the flag?" he responded. "In most cases the flag is about 15 yards from the front of the green. That in itself is almost two clubs more in distance. *Be more aggressive.* Pros win by being aggressive and you can improve your game by doing the same. That doesn't mean gambling or trying things you don't think you can do, but it does mean going for the pin at the right time rather than just hitting aimlessly at a ball.

"When you are in the rough go in there with a plan – decide what type of shot you want to hit, and where, before you start thrashing away at it, wasting strokes. Get it out first time!"

Hilversum is a parkland course which is a regular European Tour venue, often hosting the Dutch Open. It has several tight fairways with areas of woodland and rough and some heather which is nigh on impossible to get out of, Martin's advice in this situation is simple.

"Take your medicine. If you have any doubts about being able to swing the club and hit the ball cleanly back onto the fairway, pick it up, take your penalty stroke and get on with it. That way you have only dropped one shot and now have an improved lie. There's nothing brave about trying to hit shots from impossible positions. There's nothing wrong in picking up the ball. Good course management saves shots.

"Finally, get out there and practise in the rough. Ask your club professional to give you a lesson in the rough to help build your confidence. Professionals have the confidence and technique to get out – they know they will every time. Yet most amateur players are terrified of the rough – like sand – because they lack the confidence to get out. Build that confidence through practice."

Westchester, New York State, USA
Craig Watson

Using the sand wedge

"Every player has the same opportunity to get out of a hazard."

These reassuring words, giving the higher handicapper as much hope as Curtis Strange, come from Craig Watson, Director of Golf at the Westchester Golf & Country Club, a little way outside New York City.

"Whatever their playing ability and power off the tee, here in sand or long grass, they only need the right equipment and the knowledge to swing the club properly and they can get out of any hazard, putting the ball close to the pin."

It sounds too easy, doesn't it? Craig, a highly respected teacher of golf at this magnificent club and venue for the annual Westchester Open, went on to show me just how simple it really is.

"The first thing, of course, is having the right equipment. A good sand wedge is vital, for getting out of the rough as well as greenside bunkers." He went on to show me what he meant.

Craig Watson believes the right equipment for hazards is vital.

"Sand wedges are relatively new in golf, and before they were designed golfers had to use a lofted club and improvise as best they could.

"It's the *heel* of the sand wedge that is different, and which is the effective part of the club, not just the very lofted blade. A sand wedge, if swung properly, hits the sand with its heel, not the leading edge of the blade as with other clubs. It is not intended to hit the ball, but to push sand along, displacing the sand and popping the ball out on a cushion. The club-face and ball never come into direct contact.

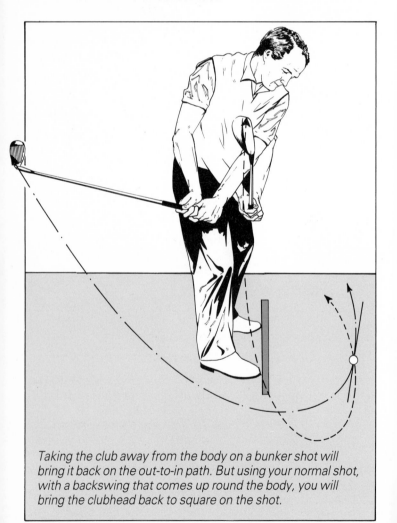

Taking the club away from the body on a bunker shot will bring it back on the out-to-in path. But using your normal shot, with a backswing that comes up round the body, you will bring the clubhead back to square on the shot.

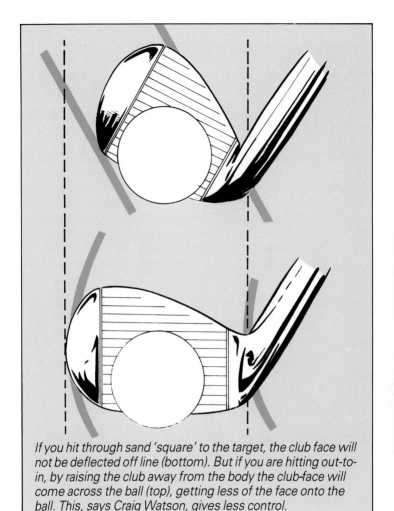

If you hit through sand 'square' to the target, the club face will not be deflected off line (bottom). But if you are hitting out-to-in, by raising the club away from the body the club-face will come across the ball (top), getting less of the face onto the ball. This, says Craig Watson, gives less control.

"If you hit in first with the leading edge of the blade all you will do is dig into the sand and probably miss the ball or fail to get it out.

"With hands and club head in line very slightly behind the ball and your weight centred, you are helping to keep the blade flatter to the surface. Thus as you swing down, the heel of the club hits first, displaces the sand and the sand pops the ball up and out."

There is, of course, a difference between greenside and fairway bunkers where you have to take the ball cleanly and you are usually aiming for distance. You would not use the sand wedge in these. In greenside bunkers, however, the object is to get the ball out high and land it softly not too far away from the pin.

"One thing I do teach here," Craig continued, "is to swing the club in sand just as you would anywhere else on the course. A lot is talked about steep takeaways and swinging on the line of the feet, swinging, in effect, in a straight line which happens to be out-to-in – providing that you stand with an open stance.

"I suggest that most players would be better off standing square or very slightly open only to encourage the player to open the club-face. Swing, as if it was any other club, pulling the club round the right shoulder on the backswing – the length depending on the power you wish to put into the shot based on the distance to go – rather than try an unusual swing path. Nobody swings out-to-in on a normal shot. Why do it here?"

We went into a bunker and Craig demonstrated clearly how a 'normal' shot would get the ball out. "It is, after all, only the

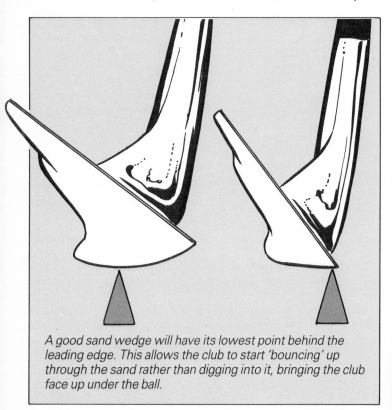

A good sand wedge will have its lowest point behind the leading edge. This allows the club to start 'bouncing' up through the sand rather than digging into it, bringing the club face up under the ball.

angle at which the club enters the sand that determines where the ball goes," he told me as I treated the bunker shot like any other, turning the shoulders as for a normal backswing.

"If you look at the path of the club coming into the sand," he said, scratching lines in the sand, "you can see that a club coming *across* the face of the ball is not going to have as large an effective hitting area for control on the ball (via the sand) as a club going *square*."

"You put extra loft onto it by opening your stance more and by keeping the club face as open as possible. But swing round, on an in-to-straight-to-in line, as for any other club."

Swinging through the target was another aspect touched on by Craig, who sees this 'quitting' fault in many high-handicap players.

"You must swing the whole way through, with the follow-through *always* being as long as the backswing. Get the club up onto that left shoulder and point to the target as you finish."

We moved out of the sand into the rough (out of the frying pan into the fire?) and continued working on the same shot out of the long grass. Again, Craig's suggestion was for a sand wedge, although obviously the choice varies with the amount of distance required.

"You can use other, less lofted clubs in the rough but if the grass is higher than the middle of the ball stay with that wedge.

"The players who score highest are often those who take longest to get out of hazards. When you're in trouble the one thing to do is to get *out!* Yet so many people forget this. They are too optimistic about their ability to hit great shots from basically terrible positions.

"Don't try to get too much out of that awkward shot. Get it back into play on the first shot. Don't turn a possible 3-shot situation into a 4-shot or 5-shot disappointment. Play safe and don't go for broke on the recovery shots – they are exactly that – 'recovery shots'.

"Many people hit one bad shot and then follow it up by hitting another, having tried the same thing twice over. In other walks of life if you fail at the first attempt you normally change the way you go about it the second time. Why should golf be any different?"

It is true that many players, having hit a bad shot or failed to get where they ought to be, stand back and mutter, "I knew that wouldn't work!" They should, as Craig so rightly points out, decide that it will not work *before* they attempt it.

As Craig so strongly advises, you should 'realise your limitations'. For anyone who has ever taken two shots to get out of a bunker or the rough, this advice is invaluable.

Royal Dublin, Republic of Ireland
Leonard Owens, Club Professional

Playing into the wind

The Royal Dublin is a true links course, nine out and nine back
with a magnificent and challenging finish. Fringing Dublin Bay
and the tempestuous Irish Sea, wind is a constant factor. It
normally comes rushing in from the south, assisting the
outward player, but what a shock when you turn and head back
in on the tenth.

The club professional is Leonard Owens, who came here in
1975 after five years on the European Tour. Leonard won the
Irish Matchplay Championship in 1972 and represented Great
Britain and Ireland at youth level. He was also a member of the
PG Club team in 1977 and 1980.

"Most golfers slice the ball, particularly into a wind," he
explained on a wonderfully windy morning, "not so much
because they are bad players but because they lead with their
hands. To hit strong and straight you must use the body,
starting the downswing with a forwards (towards the hole)
movement of the legs and hips – at the same time turning after

*The Royal Dublin is a typical links course fringed by the Irish Sea.
Playing conditions are often affected by the wind.*

An exercise to check if you are perfectly balanced at the top of the backswing. Lift your left foot off the ground completely once the club is back to the horizontal position.

impact on your left side to keep your balance.

"You have to be perfectly balanced at the top of the backswing and you can check this by lifting your left foot off the ground completely once the club is back to the horizontal position."

I tried this but nearly fell over. Leonard now uncovered a major fault in my swing; I moved my right leg on the backswing. I was *swaying* rather than turning in the legs and lower body.

He proved to me just how much I was moving by placing a club against the outside of my right leg, almost upright. As I started the backswing I knocked it over.

"Brace the lower leg more, really turning from the knee," he told me, suggesting that it was worth practising by standing with the right knee against a post. Once I had tried it a few times it became a natural feeling and made a considerable difference to the way I hit the ball – much straighter. Such a simple adjustment, yet what a big difference.

Leonard also suggested that the club only be taken back as

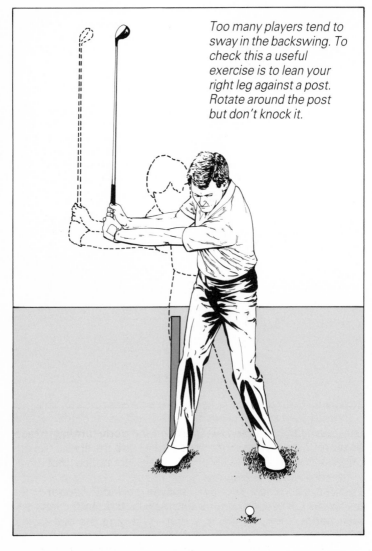

Too many players tend to sway in the backswing. To check this a useful exercise is to lean your right leg against a post. Rotate around the post but don't knock it.

far as the horizontal, which helps to maintain balance and control.

"Bend a little more at the waist," he told me, "while keeping the back straight. This will leave enough room for the hips to turn – to clear – on the backswing.

"For the most solid strike, at impact everything must be square to the target – hips, feet, knees, shoulders and club-face.

"The follow-through must be strong and long, with the club

Don't try to overhit by taking the club down the back on the backswing. To maintain control don't go past the horizontal.

being almost flung down the back and the body turning to face the target. That way you get extra power into the shot.''

If you watch short-hitters you really do notice that their follow-through ends halfway.

"When you're playing into a strong wind,'' Leonard explained as we turned into a biting gale at the tenth, "you are often better advised playing a draw, bringing the ball round right to left.

"To play a medium iron with control into the wind, aim the body slightly left of the target. Have the ball well back in the stance and swing on the line of the feet. Bring the club, naturally, out-to-in. Despite the wind don't try to over-hit it but slow the swing down even more, just accelerating the club head through the ball. Timing is more important than brute force here.

"As you begin the downswing the knees kick round even more so the body moves left towards the target, giving the impression that you are dragging the club down through the back of the ball.

"The vital thing to do here is to keep the wrists locked after impact, so that as you finish, the back of the left hand – the logo on the glove – is pointing directly up. You must not let the hands roll over into the normal follow through position."

We tried this a few times and it resulted in the ball keeping low, but long. It also moved round slightly from right to left.

Leonard explained how the hands finish here close in to the body, not extended as with other shots.

As we walked back to the club-house he told me that, for the average club golfer, he thinks metal woods are better for

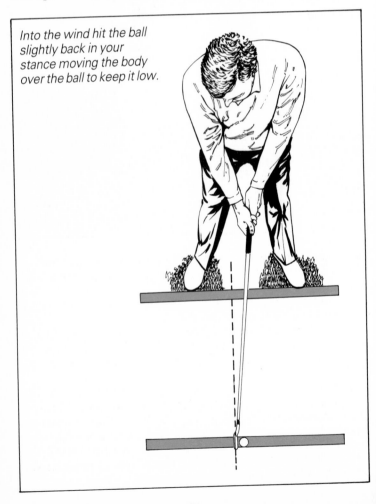

Into the wind hit the ball slightly back in your stance moving the body over the ball to keep it low.

The shot into the wind with a medium iron is more of a punch shot. Note that the wrists stay firm in the follow-through, keeping the ball down for better control.

distance off the tee, and that the offset clubs promote the hands-in-front-of-the-ball position which most golfers will find beneficial.

Equipment though, will only help the golfer who follows the five golden rules.

"One – realise you need help. Two – go to your club pro. Three – listen and learn. Four – practise until it becomes second nature. Five – use it on the course. Don't fall back into bad habits."

It is interesting to note that Royal Dublin's Touring Professional is Christy O'Connor Junior, whose splendid shot to the 18th at The Belfry during the 1989 Ryder Cup ensured that the trophy remained in Europe for the third consecutive time.

Christy O'Connor Senior has also been the club professional, and in 1966 won the Irish Open on this course by finishing with an eagle, birdie, eagle.

Ballybunion, Republic of Ireland
Ted Higgins, Club Professional

Wet weather

Ballybunion is perhaps the most famous golf course in Ireland, bordering the Atlantic Ocean. Ted Higgins is the highly respected club professional, whose teaching methods are unique and very effective.

On a wet and very windy day, with the Atlantic spray challenging players on the 7th, 11th and 16th holes in particular, he let me into the secrets of playing golf in the rain.

"There are four types of player when it comes to wet weather," he said. "The first has an umbrella, a caddy, towels and the full equipment to stay dry. The second has all the equipment but no caddy. The third has all the right equipment but doesn't look after it; and the fourth has nothing. Who do you think stands the best chance of playing well?"

The answer seemed fairly obvious.

"A caddy on a wet day is worth his weight in gold," he emphasised, pointing out that the extra assistance in keeping the clubs clean, and the grips and the player dry in inclement weather – an understatement at that particular time for the rain was coming at us almost horizontally! – gives that player an important advantage.

"But what is the right equipment?" I asked.

"Waterproof clothing, of course," he replied. "Yet it is so important to keep it in peak condition. So many people just take

Dry towels in the bag will save shots in wet conditions.

Rain suits keep the golfer warm and dry but are light and comfortable to wear. They do not greatly restrict the backswing.

off wet rain-gear, roll it up and throw it in the bag or the boot of the car, and then expect it to remain waterproof. It just cannot happen, because if you don't hang wet-weather gear up to dry in a warm place – but never in direct heat – it will lose its waterproof qualities.'' It sounds so simple yet many players neglect it.

An umbrella is essential, it goes without saying, although there may be times when it is too windy to use one.

''Having a caddy to hold the umbrella while you play a shot – but not over you as that is against the laws of golf – frees you. You don't have to close it or put it in the bag or on the ground, where it will get even wetter.

''Also, hanging inside the umbrella should be a towel, as you have probably seen at professional tournaments. This allows the player to wipe his hands before and after each shot, keeping them as dry as possible, particularly the left hand.

''Unless the left hand is dry, there is no 'feel' to a golf shot. Without that you really can't play good golf.''

Obviously that left hand, and glove, will get wet during the course of the round, with or without a caddy, so it is a good idea to take out at least three or four gloves with you. Change them and dry your hand as soon as you begin to feel uncomfortable

– or slightly before. For the player without a caddy it is obvious that a towel in the umbrella might not be the answer, as it will inevitably get wet.

"In that case keep a towel in the bag, with just a tiny bit of it showing for instant use, changing it as soon as it gets wet. A couple of clean, dry towels in the bag to change as you go round could be worth several strokes." And it is a good idea to have a towel round your neck, to stop rain dripping down your unprotected back.

The player who does not look after rain-gear, or who has wet gloves, will start feeling uncomfortable after about five holes – from then on he, or she, is constantly playing under pressure, which could have been avoided.

The player with no wet-gear, umbrella, waterproof shoes or towel is of course just wasting his money going out playing – he has no chance of playing well!

Waterproof shoes are, of course, vital, so a special pair should be bought. Normal golf shoes tend to be leather and are not waterproof – moulded shoes are.

"Providing you're dry and warm, but not too hot, playing in rain, or on wet courses, is only slightly different from any other time," Ted continued.

"Look carefully at the way the grass is growing. If it is towards the hole you have more chance of greater distance. If it's against you, less, so adjust your club either way, taking less club if it's with you, extra if against.

"If you're in thick rough in the wet, just get it back into play; don't struggle on any shot but play positive golf. In thick wet rough the grass will stop the club even more than when dry, so try to take the ball on an upswing, as cleanly as possible. If you try to dig down onto the ball the club face will close and stop, leaving you with another shot just as bad, if not worse.

"On the fairway try to take the ball a little cleaner than normal, with less divot. Get the left shoulder a little higher and aim to sweep the ball away slightly on the upswing, definitely not coming down into it. Have the ball slightly forward in the stance to hit it on the upswing.

"The greens are also slower when wet (this often happens in the morning with a heavy dew on the grass, too), so a ball aimed at the pin has less chance of bouncing on. Go for the pin.

"Above all, make sure the mind controls the shot. Think negatively and you'll hit a negative shot – think positively and you will hit a good shot far more often."

Being dressed to swing in the rain will give you several strokes advantage over someone who is not. It is an advantage that you cannot afford to ignore.

St Andrews, Scotland
Peter Tupling

Getting out of bunkers

Everybody has heard of the Hell Bunker at St Andrews, a horror of a sand pit that, when you are in it, looks like a desert stretching out in front of you and above you. It really is a fearsome place and hence its name.

Yet in reality it should present little problem for the average golfer, provided that he follows a couple of very simple rules.

My teacher early one summer's morning as the sun came up over St Andrew's Bay was Peter Tupling who spent sixteen years on the European and Safari Tours hitting a world-beating 255 in the Nigerian Open in 1981, with a 63, 66, 62, 64 (the record still stands). Peter now concentrates on teaching and runs several very successful golf schools around Europe.

Getting onto the 14th hole before play had begun on the Old Course, we dropped a number of golf balls into the notorious bunker in strategic positions. One of these Peter himself had been in during one British Open. A challenging shot for a professional yet alone a high-handicapper.

Hell Bunker is very large, almost horseshoe shaped, and fearsomely deep, the face nearest the hole being a generous nine feet, although it has been changed since the day on which Peter Tupling landed in it. Then it was ten feet deep! The ball was in the face but not plugged. However, it was sitting on the

Peter Tupling's world beating 255 in the Nigerian Open of 1981 still stands. Peter knows all about Hell Bunker at St Andrews.

steep up-slope, thus presenting a major problem to any golfer.

Peter demonstrated how he realised that it would be impossible to hit the ball out forwards, toward the hole.

"The angle was just too steep to be able to get the ball up and over the lip of the bunker," he explained, holding up a sand wedge parallel to the face of the bunker.

"*If the angle of the bunker face is steeper than that of the club the ball will not clear the bunker in that direction*," he said. The demonstration was so simple as to be obvious – yet many average golfers like myself still try to hit the ball forwards out of impossible bunker situations.

"In a case like this," he continued, "the only thing to do is to play sideways or backwards. The one thing you must do is to get the ball out of the bunker, back onto the fairway, on the *first* shot."

In that Open Peter played backwards out of the bunker, hitting the ball almost back in the direction from which it had come. He actually got into further trouble on that occasion, getting caught in another bunker cleverly positioned to catch just this type of escape shot!

"Never be afraid of hitting a ball sideways or backwards to get out of a bunker," Peter explained. And it is important to go out and look at the surrounding area to see where you would

The three positions that Peter Tupling chose in Hell Bunker. The face is about seven feet high.

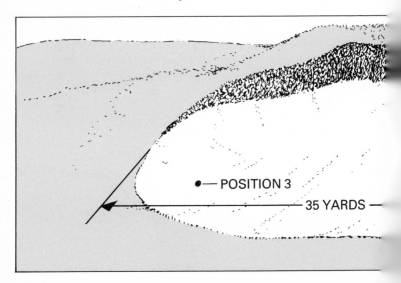

ideally like to have the ball land to give you a good next shot.

There are several ways of hitting a ball from sand, but the golden rule is to hit the sand first (except on a flat or in a fairway bunker).

"The ball comes out on a cushion of sand – if no sand comes out, no ball comes out!" He graphically illustrated this by aiming the club at the ball. It dug itself further into trouble.

"Don't even look at the ball," he told me. "Your aiming point is probably about an inch behind the ball, so look at that position in the sand."

Peter's suggestion here was to achieve a stable, balanced position from which you can safely hit the ball out of the bunker. From this position, for a right-hander, the carry has to be quite long as there are still some 30 yards of sand before you reach 'dry land'. It needed a good solid thump, but with a smooth, controlled swing with a full, high follow-through, as the club is lifting the ball out.

The second situation we tackled in the Hell Bunker was almost in the middle – still with a high face to get over but sitting up with a cushion of sand under it, not plugged.

One golden rule in bunkers (and other hazards as defined by the laws of golf) is *never to ground your club while the ball remains within the bounds of the hazard*. Quite often you see a golfer fail to clear a bunker on his first shot, then 'rake' the sand with the club, or rest it in the sand before moving to the new position for the second attempt. That, officially, is 'grounding the club' and incurs a one-stroke penalty or loss of the hole in

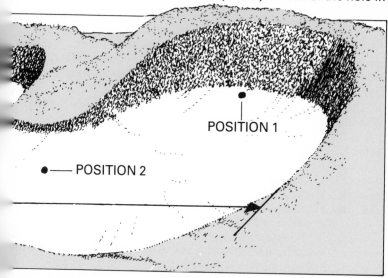

POSITION 1

POSITION 2

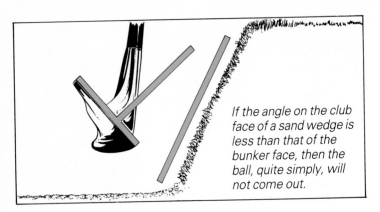

If the angle on the club face of a sand wedge is less than that of the bunker face, then the ball, quite simply, will not come out.

match play. If a rake is not to hand use your feet to 'swish' the sand back into position – it smooths the sand better than the club, which tends just to dig more holes.

"We now have a good chance of playing forward to a spot on the fairway from which our next shot becomes easier," Peter explained.

"Again, it's vital to have surveyed the scene, preferably before you even went into the bunker, to find the best position for the next shot – if you can reach it. Golf is really like a game of chess. Always plan the next move!"

Peter then demonstrated the correct way to get out of a bunker. The stance was very open, with the ball off the left toe. The club, held almost flat, but not touching the sand, had its shaft pointing almost directly at the belt buckle, the hands well up on the shaft. For someone who had always gripped 'down' for control in bunkers the position felt strange when I tried it.

"Swing steeply, and swing on the line of the feet," Peter emphasised. I did so, hitting half an inch behind the ball, maintaining a balanced position and swinging with the arms, keeping the legs and lower body still.

"Don't be too concerned about turning; this is a short shot where you need control, not distance."

The ball flipped out high and soft, and landed well on the safe part of the fairway. My next shot to the green was much easier.

The set-up had felt awkard and clumsy, as if I had no control over the club, but the swing, once you have tried it a few times, becomes quite natural. How simple it is to change old habits – and how difficult!

Peter then explained his Triangle Theory for bunker play.

"For a long bunker shot, where the aim is distance, not height (from a fairway bunker, for example) the triangle made by the feet and direction of ball is fairly flat and narrow. For a short shot, where we are aiming to get the ball up high and land it softly, the triangle is wide and stubby."

The important thing, though, is to lift the club back steeply, not going back over the shoulders, so there is little body turn. Swing on the line of the feet, almost straight through, particularly for a short shot. Use the power of the hands and arms, not the body.

The third bunker position was easier.

The ball was sitting up near the back of the bunker, with a clear view of the flag about 120 yards away.

"Here," said Peter, "the situation is totally different. The face of the bunker is no longer a problem, and we want to hit the ball away cleanly, for distance, not just height. Imagine, then, that it's a normal fairway shot, so you need to hit the ball first, not the sand."

I reached instinctively for a sand wedge. Wrong! "Try a seven," suggested Peter. Now for 120 yards a 7-iron would be far too much club for the average player. I voiced my opinion but was told to try it.

I did, probably holding back for fear of going halfway up the fifteenth. The shot was firm, but with only a half-swing. Sure enough, it stopped thirty yards short.

The next time I swung fuller, not quite full because I was keeping the feet and lower body still, with only a slight shoulder turn. That is enough to remove distance, and with a three-quarter swing the ball popped up nicely and flew to the front of the green, landing just off the fringe and rolling to within six inches of the pin. Had it been Greg Norman in the Open there would have been a thunderous roar of approval. As it was, two seagulls, preening themselves on the green, were startled by the arrival of a ball this early in the day and leapt into the air, screeching angrily at the intrusion.

Oh well, you can't win them all!

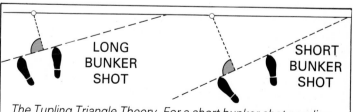

LONG BUNKER SHOT

SHORT BUNKER SHOT

The Tupling Triangle Theory. For a short bunker shot needing height, adopt a very open stance and swing along the feet line. For a longer bunker shot, have a less open stance. Always be sure the ball is positioned correctly.

Rapallo, Italy
Andrea Canessa, Professional

Only drop one shot in a hazard

Having learnt from Jennifer Lawrence, a player on the WPGA Tour, how to play high shots over hazards, I thought it only fair to include one of the players on the Men's Tour. Seeking the sun on a January morning I headed south to the Mediterranean coast of Italy, and to the small town of Rapallo.

My host was Andrea Canessa, a European Tour player, whose father, Manuel Canessa, is the head professional at the beautifully laid out Rapallo Golf Club.

"The most important thing for an average-handicap player to remember," Andrea told me as we walked out onto the long par-5 2nd, "is to avoid the trees and rough. Tournament players don't find themselves off the fairway too often, but handicap players need not stray too far either by asking too much of themselves in the first place."

Tour players, he explained, have far greater control over the ball and can, therefore, hit it to much tighter targets. Sometimes, of course, they miss, but that is the exception rather than the rule, and even then they normally only find themselves a few yards off the edge. The average player should, then, give himself or herself a far greater chance of keeping the ball on the fairway by *aiming at a bigger target*, and *not straining too much for distance* with a subsequent loss of control. By having a bigger target area to aim at, you improve your chances of hitting it, rather than having to worry about squeezing a ball tight in to the side and risking missing the fairway completely.

Think how much easier it is to hit the ball straight on the driving range than off the first tee! The target is bigger; the player therefore does not feel under such stress to hit an imaginary target.

"If you are in the rough, or the trees, though," says Andrea, "think only of getting the ball out, but to a place on the fairway from where your next shot will be easy with no hazards in the way. Only ever drop *one* shot in a hazard – never risk dropping two shots."

For Tour players like Andrea, the ball in the rough demands a particular type of shot. He personally favours a 5-wood to part the grass and get the ball airborne (for a fairly long shot

Andrea Canessa, Professional at Rapallo Golf Club. If the ball is tight against the back lip of a bunker, a strong player might be able to hit down through the grass, cutting through it to get under the ball.

naturally, not a short one). The lie of the ball, however, is the decisive factor.

"I would never use more than a 5- or 6-iron. Talk of hitting a 2-iron 200 yards out of the rough is just a fairy-story. Just get *out* of the rough, first time. It is also vital that you carefully choose the spot on the fairway from which you would like to hit your next shot. Play chess with the ball."

We moved on closer to the green, finding one of those wonderful bunkers that is bowl-shaped. A month or so previously, I had encountered a really difficult shot that I could not figure out. I now asked Andrea to help.

The ball had been lying right up tight against the back edge, a downslope in front of it, and a steep lip to get over to the flag

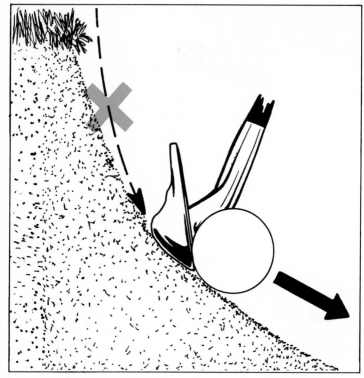

In this situation it is impossible to hit down on the ball as the club would bounce off the grass at the top of the bunker, and could not strike the ball.

which was positioned only 10 yards in from the edge.

Trying to hit down on it was impossible as the club would just bounce off the grass behind the ball. Andrea told me what he would do in a tournament.

''There are three possibilities – and the amateur player has the same choice. Firstly, if you are physically strong enough, hit down into the back of the ball through the grass, taking a huge chunk of grass out from the bunker edge. To set up you can ground the club outside the bunker and I would use a sand wedge to literally cut through the bank and hit into the back of the ball. However, you do need to be very strong.

''Secondly, I could try to squeeze the ball out from the bank, with a 6-iron, running it through the bunker and up onto the green. But if the lip is very steep this might not work.

''Thirdly, and safest, is to hit out sideways or backwards, to a position from where you can play a little chip and run to the pin.

The safest option with a lie like this might be to hit out sideways. When the ball rests against an obstacle, address it on the toe of the club, the broadest part. That way you have a better chance of connecting properly with it.

Do remember that, unless there is a hazard in the way, the average player is better off playing chip-and-run shots than pitching. They're easier to judge.

"When you are chipping out sideways from a bunker with the ball up against the back lip there is a sure way of ensuring proper contact to get the ball out to where you want it."

Andrea then proceeded to show me how.

"Have the ball positioned just outside the right foot with a square stance to your intended target. Address the ball with the *toe* of the club, remembering not to ground it in the bunker, and have the club-face closed."

Having the face closed reduces the club's tendency to bounce, making it dig in deeper and punch the ball out.

"Keep your weight all on the left side, with the hands and wrists cocked – don't alter their angle during the fairly short backswing. Keep the body still, dragging the club through with the arms. The hands are obviously well in front of the ball."

I tried the shot and was surprised to see how the club face did dig in, lifting the ball out but continuing to dig in until it came to a stop. There is no follow-through and this must be a reaction to the club digging in. Under no circumstances must you think about *not* following through or you will slow the club down as you come into the sand. You must aim to follow through, swinging smoothly as you would normally. Do not think about open stance or closed stance – swing straight through on the line of the feet, which should be aimed at your target.

We then moved across the bunker to that treacherous lip, a steep upslope that looked as if crampons might be needed to get up it. We threw the ball in hard, plugging it.

To get a shot at the ball, Andrea had to perch one leg over the top of the bunker, and plant the other firmly in the sand on the upslope, digging in until he got a very firm foothold.

"For this shot, balance is everything," he said. "Lock that right leg in with the weight firmly on it and stay still throughout the shot. If you lose your balance you will miss the ball.

"Use a sand wedge, again having it slightly closed, to dig in under the ball and pop it up and out over the lip. How high you hit it depends on the condition of the green, any slopes on the green and where exactly the pin is. From this position you can't do much more than just hit the ball straight up in the air. This really is quite an easy shot if your target is no more than getting out of trouble.

"A plugged ball is very hard to play but on a long bunker shot can sometimes be more controllable than one that is sitting up. The ball that is sitting up has to be hit directly underneath it and so will have a lot of backspin. That's fine for a short shot out of

This shot requires some acrobatics. All the weight is held vertically over the right leg. Grip down the shaft and be sure the clubhead hits into the sand almost horizontally, popping the ball gently into the air.

sand that you want to bite as it hits the green. But for the longer shot, having the sand between the club and ball reduces backspin and will keep the ball rolling. A ball sitting up in sand has to be hit very precisely — one plugged can be lifted out easier because of the sand.''

Mastery out of sand is one skill that separates the professionals from the rest of us. But forethought about what you are trying to do can save you strokes, to say nothing of embarrassment — provided, of course, that you know what you are supposed to be trying to do. Learning from the professionals what you want to do is, quite simply, the answer. That, and practice.

Hartford TPC, Connecticut, USA

JR Weidinger, Professional

Psychological hazards

The view from the 17th tee at Hartford is daunting. From an elevated position the lake dominates the scene in front of you, a seemingly tiny landing area which passes as a fairway away to the left bounded by huge mounds. Here, during the Hartford Open in March, up to 50,000 people can be perched, watching every movement the golfer makes. Away to the right across the lake is the tiny green.

The slightest error means at least one dropped shot and maybe the loss of the tournament, for after this there is precious little time to make up for mistakes – just one difficult par-5 to finish. Professionals on the US Tour have to contend with these types of pressure week in, week out.

The temptation here is to try cutting corners rather than simply to play safe. The slightest error means at least one dropped shot. 'Why dice with danger?' asks JR Weidinger.

Take away the crowds, the television and the vast amounts of prize money, but put in personal pride and you have the situation that confronts every golfer who plays this difficult course, the back nine of which are totally different in character from the front.

"The hazard here," said JR Weidinger, recently head golf professional at Hartford, "is a *psychological* one." And it is a hazard that comes into the game every time you play, whether it be a particular type of shot, as from sand, or a specific hole that always gives you a problem.

On one course that I play regularly in the UK there is a simple 154 yard par-3 that always causes me distress. The narrow green is elevated with steep bunkers either side; miss the centre of the green and you can waste half a dozen shots going from one bunker to the next. I have never got down in less than five and as a result am terrified by it.

JR (it is John Ross really but he has always been known as JR, long before Dallas) has some good advice for this type of situation which we all face at least once on every round when we come to a hole, or a shot, that we feel we might foul up.

"If you're going to miss, miss on the safe side," advised JR.

"However," he continued, "you must really channel your thoughts on where you want the ball to land. Negative thinking will lead to negative results."

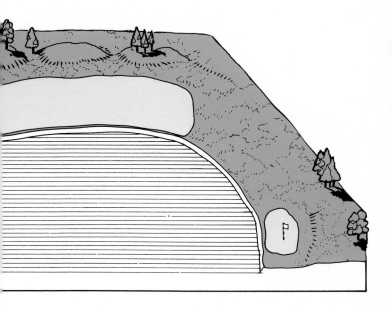

The hazard here is a psychological one. It is easy to look at the huge lake rather than the fairway but the secret is to simply ignore the hazard.

As we stood on the tee he explained how, here, he would totally ignore the lake, looking, and concentrating, on the fairway to the left.

"If you do miss here, miss on the left where there is safety. Take that safe side – why dice with danger?"

Missing on the right will mean a lost ball!

"Before I even get to the course I am playing my round," he told me. "You've heard of visualizing shots, but you need to go

72

further and understand exactly what you want the ball to do to give you your *next* shot.

"Don't worry too much about visualizing the way the ball will fly up, or the swing. Just concentrate on where the ball is to land. And always take one *specific*, reachable target. Be precise in your thoughts – your aim will follow them."

When we moved down to the fairway, which was a much larger landing area than it had looked 200 yards back up the hill, we were then faced with a difficult shot across the lake, of some 140 yards.

"Again," JR emphasized, "you must concentrate on the positive. If you're looking at the lake thinking, 'If I hit a really good shot it will probably just make it across', the chances are that you won't make it.

"If you think you have to hit a special shot, forget it – play safe. When you're under extra psychological pressure, like carrying across a lake, you will be more tense in your swing. Given an ordinary fairway you probably could hit a further 200 yards. But when you have that extra concern about water – which all players have – you will be concentrating too much on swinging differently or extra powerfully to get the ball across.

"If you have to hit a special shot, don't bother. Go the safe route. Do it with a normal shot, or don't do it!

"The same goes for those little approach shots," he continued. "You're faced with that chip or pitch decision.

"First, decide what you want to achieve. Do you want the ball to carry a small area and then run to the pin, or do you want to fly it the whole way? A pitch has maximum air time, minimum ground time. A chip has the opposite: maximum ground time, minimum air time. Each requires a different technique, so make up your mind before you hit the shot, not after.

"The same applies to that most difficult area – putting. Many players, including top-class professionals, occasionally suffer the 'yips' – they stand over a putt and just can't sink it.

"Too many amateur players worry about missing the hole on the 'professional' side rather than the 'amateur' side. But why worry about *missing* it?

"Putting is one area where you really can improve your game by practising," JR contends. "It is, after all, almost fifty per cent of your game. Yet how much time do you give it? Most guys are quite happy to go to the driving range and blast shots 200 yards. But confidence in putting, which comes from practice, will knock several strokes off each round, without having to be a big hitter!

"Practise putting until you drop. Start with one-foot putts, and knock ten in out of ten. Then move back to two-footers and do the same, until you never miss. Go uphill, downhill, across. Then move right back to the edge of the green and just roll them to within two feet of the hole. That way you should never more than two-putt.

"Practice builds confidence, and as about seventy per cent of the game of golf is played with less than full swings, it's pretty obvious where you should spend time on your game."

That confidence around the green will definitely pay dividends, cutting several wasted strokes off your round. Yet not everyone wants to practise.

"No," he agreed, "so you need to fix your goals clearly. If you just want to go out, hit a few balls and drink some beer with the guys, that's fine. But for anyone who wants to improve and enjoy their golf, practice is necessary. And most people agree that the better they play the more they enjoy themselves.

"Golf is fun – have fun, but most important of all, concentrate your mind on the possible. Block out hazards. Don't even think of hitting into them."

Now where's that par-3 I was telling you about?

Many of us try too hard on difficult shots. With a shot like this across water, many players would hit harder and faster to carry the lake. Better to keep your rhythm.

Pymble G.C.,
Sydney, Australia
Ian Paul, Club Professional

Hot weather

What a scorcher! The temperature had rocketed to 32°C (90°F), the sun burning down out of a cloudless blue sky, with not a breath of wind. It was the sort of day to head for the beach and lay basking on the golden sand. But the only sand around me was that in the bunker on one of the finest golf courses to the north of Sydney – Pymble.

The professional, Ian Paul, had met me in the bar. I asked Ian how best to cope with such torrid conditions on the golf course.

"The most important thing to remember in hot weather is to drink a lot. Dehydration can be a very serious problem, particularly for senior players or those with heart problems. You really do need to drink as much as you can to maintain your body fluid level."

Ian went on to point out that alcohol is *not* the thing to drink – not until the 19th anyway! – as it just adds to your dehydration problems.

"Personally," he told me, "I prefer a soft drink – if one is available – or just water."

Some golf courses have fountains or water dispensers. Making use of them will help you remain comfortable and safer. Drinking after every couple of holes will definitely help you retain your concentration as well as your health. For clubs without water fountains you may need to take a stock of drink out with you during your round.

"Correct UV (ultra violet) screen sun lotion should also be applied on exposed parts of the body, particularly arms, face and neck. That will help prevent soreness, burning and perhaps even skin cancer."

Skin cancer is one of the principal causes of death in Australia, but playing in any hot sun close to the tropics can put you at risk – unless you are effectively protected with a sun block or protective sunscreen.

Many of the senior players on the course on the day of my visit were sensibly wearing long-sleeved shirts to protect them from the burning sun. Indeed, I was surprised to learn that many of them were in fact already victims of skin cancer in varying degrees.

"Hats offer most protection though," Ian told me, who was sporting one himself. "Shorts help you to stay cool, but only if

you're used to wearing them – otherwise the backs of your leg
will burn.''

Many golf clubs these days allow shorts in hot weather
provided that they are of the tailored variety.

Apart from clothing you need to have some extra care fo
your clubs. A towel – wet at one end – is essential to wipe th
club face after every shot, keeping it clean from grass tha
would have an adverse effect on your play.

Grips need wiping regularly, depending, of course, on th
degree to which your hands perspire.

Gloves should, if possible, be changed during the round, and
it will help if you take your glove off between shots.

''I recommend all-weather gloves for the average clu
golfer,'' Ian told me. ''Buying leather gloves all the time can b

*Ian Paul, Club Professional at Pymble, warns against dehydration
when playing in hot weather. It is important to maintain your body
fluid level. Hats are also highly recommended.*

The clubhouse at Pymble, which is one of the finest courses to be found in Australia north of Sydney.

expensive as they can't be washed. All-weather ones can."

"What about the hard greens?" I asked. "How can you control the ball?"

"This comes down to economics," Ian replied. "With the two-piece surlyn cover ball it is almost impossible to stop it. Even the tour pros would find it difficult.

"To control the ball you need either a wound ball, which is very difficult to find – or a balata ball. It's the only way. Yet obviously balata balls are expensive and cut much easier. Once cut, they're useless."

Playing golf in hot weather can be much more uncomfortable than it need be. If you are *not* comfortable you will find concentration more difficult and higher scoring more likely. So remember to take the simple and easy precautions that Ian strongly recommends.

16

Augusta National, USA
Bob Kletcke, Club Professional

Dealing with tall trees

Augusta National has been described as 'a dream course in a dream setting' but both the course and clubhouse are strictly off-limits to any but members and their personal guests — except, that is, at Masters time, when there is a scramble for tickets. This top US golf tournament has been won by some of the great names in golf including Nelson, Snead, Hogan, Player and, more recently, Faldo and Lyle.

"It's essential to be aware of the need to get in a good tee-shot," Bob Kletcke, the professional told me as we stood on the tee of the 17th. This uphill hole is totally dominated by the famous 'Eisenhower Tree', a huge – and still growing – Georgia Pine. It acquired its name from the much-loved World War II

A view of the fairway on the 17th. The course was designed by Bobby Jones, one of the great figures in golf. He was helped in the design by Alistair MacKenzie, a Scottish born physician who abandoned medicine to concentrate on golf.

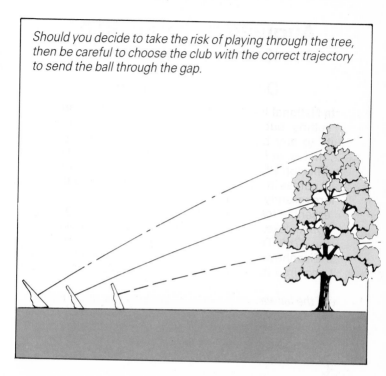

Should you decide to take the risk of playing through the tree, then be careful to choose the club with the correct trajectory to send the ball through the gap.

General who went on to hold the highest office in the land from 1953 to 1961. 'Ike' often played at Augusta National, the most prestigious club in the United States, and hit the tree almost every time he played. He is reported not only to have threatened to have it cut down but to have promised to come out in a thunderstorm and place several bags of clubs under the tree in the hope that lightning might destroy it!

However, the tree has survived Ike's battering and countless thunderstorms and stands today bigger than ever, now some 70 feet tall and getting so 'bushy' that the club may have to begin trimming it out in a year or two.

"For the moment, though, it is the dominant feature on the hole," Bob told me, "so it is vital to get in a good drive." The pros here in the Masters tend to go over it, but the members, who are playing from a tee only about 125 yards away, need to go round it because of its height. Only those better players who can safely carry a ball over 200 yards, with height, should attempt to go over the top.

"The average player should aim to go right of the tree, but preferably with hook, never slice. The next problem, of course, is that the hole leads fairly steeply uphill for the first 200 yards,

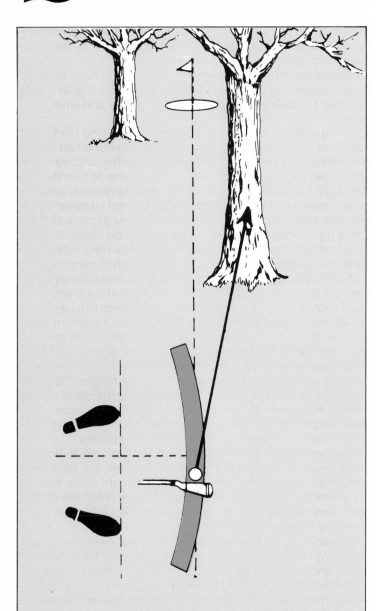

Be careful when aiming if you have to play out low between trees. Playing the ball back in your stance will have the effect of sending the ball further to the right, so make sure you allow for this.

so that shot is uphill too, making it more difficult to get roll. The fairways here are so lush that there tends not to be much forward roll once the ball lands."

It is essential, therefore, to get that first shot in *high*, to get as much 'air-time' as possible. Teeing up slightly higher might help, but the swing needs to be just as gentle and smooth as ever.

Hitting a ball with hook, or 'draw', entails closing the face of the driver or 3-wood slightly, aiming left of your direct line to the safe landing area. By standing with your feet aligned to the first target, and the club at the second, you should turn the ball in mid-air, having first started the ball in a straight line. Judging it right means that the ball passes the tree and lands safely on the other side – but judging it right is what the game is about.

Having – hopefully– missed the tree, the next obstacle, apart from that uphill shot, is a line of trees on the right side of the fairway beginning some 60 yards after the infamous pine.

The shot to the green must be kept left to avoid not only those trees but also a large bunker to the front right of the green. With a first shot of, say, 175 yards, the next shot needs to be aimed at the left side of the fairway either laying up for a pitch on and a possible five, or, for the longer-drive and better-iron (or long wood off the fairway) player, going for the green. But in the latter case the left side is the only safe route in. For the player who has made 175 yards on the first shot a further 200 yards await him, so that middle-iron to the safe area in front of the left side of the green is the sensible shot. This is better than straining and maybe missing the fairway altogether, which is likely to happen when you overstretch your abilities.

The green itself, like so many at Augusta National, is difficult, being anything but flat. This one slopes from the back right corner to the front left, making missing the pin at the front of the green, for an uphill putt, the safe option. With the greens being very fast any downhill putt is a gamble. Going uphill you definitely have more control.

The tricks on this hole to catch the unwary, or foolhardy, are testimony to the brilliance of the course's designer, the legendary Bobby Jones, who also lived here, in a cottage just off the tenth fairway, during his later life. Ike, too, had a 'cabin', though it was and is more like a mini-palace, named, inevitably, 'The White House' by the staff.

Bob Kletcke himself came to Augusta in 1962, shortly after Ike stepped down from the Presidency. He has played with and helped, many of the of the members since then, including the ex-President. To all of them who ask how to play the 17th, Bob has the same response – '*Get the drive in!*'

Kingswood, Surrey, UK
Jennifer Lawrence, Tour Professional

The pre-shot routine

"Adopt a routine before you make *any* shot."

The words of wisdom – and experience – come from Jennifer Lawrence, a European Tour (Ladies) player and a teacher at her own club, Kingswood, and at other clubs in Surrey and in Continental Europe.

Jennifer has been on the European Tour since 1982 so she knows well the rigours of travel and battling for prize-money. She also runs very successful golf days for companies and golf societies, using other members of the WPGA Tour in pro-ams.

All tournament professionals need to be attached to a particular club. Jennifer's, Kingswood, is set in glorious woodland on top of the North Downs, a beautiful part of Surrey, south of London. The course is laid out on the side of a hill, so sloping lies are the rule rather than the exception and the ball needs to be hit to one side of the fairway on almost every shot.

The final eighteenth hole finishes back outside the white-walled club-house, and the fairway is, on the right-hand side, lined with trees. Not huge trees as I experienced at St Pierre, but these are younger, thinner ones that leave the wayward

Jennifer Lawrence, a European Tour (Ladies) player and a teacher at Kingswood and other English and European clubs.

A view of the final eighteenth hole at Kingswood. The course is set in some beautiful woodland.

player like myself with the option of playing over them as well as round them. In fact, if you are far enough away from the trees, the 'over-the-top' route is the safest and straightest.

But before hitting over the top, or at least attempting to do so, back to Jennifer's pre-shot routine.

"There are six things to do before hitting any shot. If you can get into the habit of doing them before every shot you will be eliminating some of the problems in your game," Jennifer continued.

"Having a standard routine helps you to spend more time concentrating on the shot and less time worrying about stance, grip, backswing and everything else.

"The first thing is to take aim. You'll notice that all top professionals approach the ball from the back, looking over the ball to the target. That gives them a perfect view of the line of flight. Then, of course, you circle round to the side of the ball and aim the club, with the base of the club face square to the target. Unless the club face is aimed correctly you won't be able to hit the target.

"Point two is to grip the club. Having the correct grip is vital – without that you will never play good golf."

There are three main grip types: the popular Vardon grip; the interlocking grip; and the ten-finger grip for players with small hands, or those who just prefer to have all their fingers on the grip. I am in the last category, although I have experimented with the interlocking grip.

Jennifer showed me how to take the correct grip on the club. Having aimed the club-face, the club is left in position and the hands relaxed – she even suggests just shaking the left hand to ensure that it is not tensed at all.

"Once you are relaxed, and with the club still aimed correctly, place the left hand on the club, the shaft running across from the base of the index finger to the pad opposite the thumb. The left thumb is then placed on the front of the shaft, but very slightly to the right so that the 'V' formed by the thumb and index finger is pointing at the right shoulder. Then wrap the fingers around the club, feeling comfortable with not too much pressure.

"The right hand then joins the left, the little finger of the right hand overlapping – or interlocking – the index finger of the left." With my ten-finger grip the fingers are pushed up really

To hit the ball high, open the clubface as much as possible and have an open stance. Swing along the feet line rather than the ball-to-target line.

OUT-TO-IN
BALL-TO-TARGET

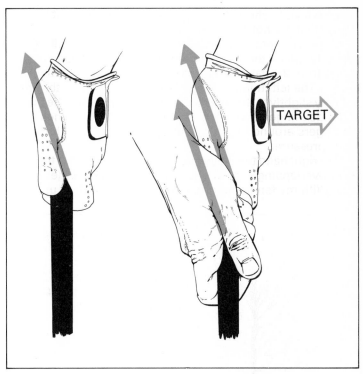

TARGET

The Grip. Place the thumb of the left hand on the front of the shaft so that the V formed by the thumb and index finger points at the right shoulder. The right hand then joins the left.

snugly against each other without overlapping. The feeling is the same in each case – the hands feel 'fitted' together.

"Both the 'Vs' should be point in the same direction."

You can practise getting the grip right at home. Stand in front of a long mirror just gripping and releasing the club, until you can get it in the perfect position every time. This can have a major impact on your golf.

Jennifer then moved on to the next golden rule

"The position of the ball is important," she told me. "For a drive it needs to be off the left instep and progressively further back for each club. Again this is something you can practise almost anywhere."

As we were going to hit over some trees with a 7-iron to the green, the ball needed to be in the middle of the stance.

"Body alignment is also very important. You must be balanced on your feet, having them wide enough apart to

The follow-through stops with the club pointing along the 'body' target line. You should have the feeling that you are throwing the club underarm. The swing should be slow and smooth.

maintain your balance during the swing. The body should, like the club face, be parallel to the ball-to-target line.''

It is worth noting here that the body's target may be different from that of the club face. In the position we were in, I needed to stand open (left foot further back than the right) to enhance the loft of the club, clipping the ball high over the trees.

Posture is the fifth rule.

''You must be balanced and yet not too tense to be able to swing, twisting and turning as you do so. Your knees should be bent just enough for you to be able to swing freely without having to stretch for the ball.''

The sixth part of the pre-shot routine is the swing itself – or rather the backswing – for after you've hit the ball there is not a lot you can do to correct any faults. Follow-through is important, too, because it ensures that the club is not being decellerated through the ball but is hitting through it.

Jennifer corrected one of my faults which I'm sure I share with many other players. As I began the backswing, right on the take-away, I very slightly 'cocked' my wrists, lifting the club a tiny fraction out of line.

"Unless you start the take-away with firm wrists, you won't get back to the ball square," Jennifer explained. "You should feel that the take-away begins not with the hands or wrists but with the right shoulder. Just keep everything else still and begin to pull the right shoulder back."

It promotes a better turn, keeps the club face square and will bring the club back to the ball in the same position in which it started – provided that you don't do anything else wrong in the backswing. Again this is something to practise standing in front of a mirror until you get it right. Your muscles will then remember the feel of the right way. Golf is repetitive in the body movements – get them right by training your body to 'feel' them.

We continued with the matter of hitting a ball high over the nearby trees to the green, using a 7-iron.

"From here the distance is possibly the same as a 9-iron hit straight, but you need to put extra height on the ball so it will not travel as far. Thus you must take extra club to get that distance," Jennifer continued.

"Adopt an open stance, keep the ball slightly forward in the stance and aim the body, and thus the club's swing path, left of the target. As you come across the ball you will automatically fade it, providing the club-face is square to the real ball-to-target line – in this instance the pin."

The swing path on this shot, and for the pitching wedge we hit as we moved closer to the green, but still with trees between us and the green, is steeper, coming into the ball from out-to-in.

Jennifer emphasised the importance of the follow-through on all these shots, particularly when you want to hit a high ball. That 'lazy' swing, slow and yet smooth, with a high finish, helps put height on the ball, which in turn brings it down softly with not too much forward roll on the green, so any shot like this should be aimed directly at the pin.

The follow-through should have the feeling that you are throwing the ball at the target, but gently, slowly. This helps yet to get the body into the right position, turned to face the target.

Being on the European Tour, Jennifer regularly plays the best courses in Europe. I asked her whether she visualized her round as some other professionals have advocated.

"Yes, but I do it three holes at a time," she told me. "I think of the first three holes and work out exactly what shots I need to score well and then go out to try to do it. Then I have in mind what the next three holes will play like. If I tried all eighteen in one go I would end up confused.

And before every shot Jennifer, like many top professionals, has her set, six-point routine.

Caring for your Clubs

For most people a set of golf clubs represents a fairly major investment, particularly if the shafts are graphite. With a full set of irons, three woods (or metal woods), golf bag, and footwear and clothing, the average player will have spent more than when buying a top quality washing machine, video or colour television.

Yet it is amazing how badly some people treat their clubs. Even more surprising is the way that most of them stand up to the sort of maltreatment that they often receive.

Kept well and maintained properly a good set of golf clubs could last a lifetime – though certain repairs will be needed in that time.

The most important thing is to keep the clubs clean. If you ever look at a professional's clubs during a tournament you will notice that they are spotless. After every shot the caddy will wipe the club face to get rid of any mud or grass which could affect the next shot. Having mud or grass caked on the club face is like driving a car with bald tyres; there is just no grip.

You, too, can ensure that your clubfaces are clean by simply wiping them with the towel hanging from the side of the bag. It is a good idea to wet the end of this towel before you start your round and to keep it damp, particularly if the weather is dry.

After a round of golf, clean your clubs thoroughly, using a nylon nail brush to clean the grooves, and plenty of cold water. Also dry the grips if they are wet. Clean the grips with soap and water after every few games; this will stop them from getting sticky and soiled. Leave them out of the bag until they are thoroughly dry.

Grips should be changed when they become worn otherwise they too will lose their adhesion and you will feel the club slipping in your fingers. A general rule is to change them after every fifty to seventy games, though some wear faster than others. New grips can be fitted by your club professional relatively inexpensively and you will notice an immediate difference in your game.

Perhaps the worst thing for golf clubs is salt – it eats through them and rots them. If you drive your car in the winter, when salt is put on roads to keep ice away, you will, if you are careful, have the car cleaned to get rid of the corrosive salt. Golf clubs also corrode so you should wash them completely – every club

– after a game on any seaside links course. You will be surprised at how much salt is in the air, and thus on your clubs.

Club technology has moved on enormously over the past few years and will, no doubt, continue to develop as golf ball design has reached its legal limits. My own clubs have shafts of graphite and boron. These, and other similar materials, need cleaning in the same way as steel.

One slight problem with graphite mixture shafts is that they will 'ring' where they touch the side of the golf bag. The friction will leave a small white ring on the shaft, which is unsightly and will affect its performance. Most manufacturers are still trying to come up with a totally reliable solution to this problem. You can avoid it by fixing a piece of masking tape around the shaft where it rubs on the side of the bag. I have taped the bottom six inches or so of all my shafts, obviously extending up the shaft with the longer irons. It does not affect the feel of the club and is legal – it is only illegal if you alter them *during* a round.

The other major danger for graphite is the use of those tubes that you see in some bags. The tubes will ruin graphite shafts in under a year.

Woods need very careful attention and I suggest that you have them revarnished every year to keep them in top condition. Metal woods, however, need only the same attention as the irons. Again if you use graphite shafts, then protect them with the special, long head covers.

Golf bags themselves are mostly made of plastic materials and can be wiped clean with a damp cloth.

Finally, if you travel with your clubs overseas – and mine go all round the world with me regularly – protect them properly with a bag cover and a golf bag carrier. I also cover the club heads themselves with an extra layer of towelling wrapped round the clubs. Lock the bags carefully – my experiences with airports and baggage handlers would make many grown men break down and cry.

Look after your clubs – and they will look after you!

Scoring

In the United States there are special score-cards on the market to help players understand their game better. They are extremely useful. Opposite is an example of a score-card that will help you improve your game. Next time you play, use this card, take the notes down as indicated, and you will understand your game better. You will also need to spend some time on a practice area measuring the distances you hit with each club. I suggest you hit six balls with each club, off a decent lie, in good conditions (i.e. not strong wind or rain) starting with the sand wedge.

Have one target in mind, a distant landmark out of reach, but aim every shot in the same direction and hit it normally – do not give it everything. You should not be trying to get an 8-iron 200 yards, like Sandy Lyle or Greg Norman – if you hit it 100 yards that's fine. The idea is to know how far you hit it on average – not your best shot, nor the one you top and send 45 yards. Ignoring the longest and the shortest, you should end up with three or four balls grouped together within approximately a ten-yard radius.

Pace the distance out, or measure it accurately, and make a note of it. Repeat the process for every club in the bag.

You will then know your average achievable distance with each club. Take into account any wind or other climatic conditions, the state of the fairways (on hard ground you get more roll, so greater distance), and whether the shot is uphill or down hill and you will know which club you should be using. Never go for the career-best shot – play average golf. It pays.

Now by using the scorecard on page 95, you will be able to analyse your game, working out where you went wrong, or where you improved on your normal performance. Spend some time practising on your weaker areas and your golf will improve.

Sounds easy? It is. So easy and simple you've probably never thought of it before. When you do go to your club pro for a lesson you can show him what type of a game you are playing and ask for his help on those areas needing a little work. If you go to a doctor or physiotherapist, you start by telling him or her you have a pain in the leg, arm, back, head or wherever. It's a starting point. So it is with golf. Know where you need help and you're half way there.

Course: North Hampshire Golf Club, UK. December 29th 1989.
Weather: cold (4°C), breezy and dry but overcast.

Key	Clubs:
Holes show as:	SW = Sand Wedge, PW = Pitching Wedge.
No. 1	Shots:
par 4	Length: L–Long; M–Medium; Sh–Short
yards 264	Position: L–Left; C–Centre; R–Right
index 18	(of target aimed at, not pin)

Hole	Shot	Club	Length L	Length M	Length S	Position L	Position C	Position R	Happy/ Unhappy
1	1	3-wood	★				★		Happy
par 4	2	8-iron		★		★			Unhappy
264 –	3	putter	★					★	Unhappy
18	4	putter			★		★		Unhappy
	5	putter		★					Happy
2	1	3-wood			★	★			Unhappy
par 4	2	5-iron	★				★		Happy
445 –	3	7-iron			★				Unhappy
3	4	SW						★	Unhappy
	5	putter		★			★		Happy
3	1	3-wood		★		★			Happy
par 4	2	5-iron		★			★		Happy
351 –	3	8-iron			★	★			Unhappy
12	4	putter			★			★	Happy
	5	putter		★			★		Happy
4	1	5-iron		★				★	Unhappy
par 3	2	putter			★		★		Unhappy
150 –	3	putter		★			★		Happy
14									
5	1	1-wood		★			★		Happy
par 4	2	4-iron		★			★		Unhappy
426 –	3	SW			★		★		Unhappy
2	4	putter			★		★		Unhappy
	5	putter		★			★		Happy

Hole	Shot	Club	Length L	M	S	Position L	C	R	Happy/Unhappy
6 par 4 356 – 9	1	3-wood	★			★			Unhappy
	2	9-iron		★			★		Happy
	3	SW			★		★		Unhappy
	4	putter			★	★			Happy
	5	putter		★			★		Happy
7 par 4 412 – 7	1	3-wood			★			★	Unhappy
	2	7-iron	★				★		Happy
	3	7-iron		★				★	Unhappy
	4	8-iron			★		★		Unhappy
	5	putter		★			★		Happy
8 par 3 124 – 16	1	8-iron		★				★	Happy
	2	putter			★			★	Happy
	3	putter		★			★		Happy
9 par 4 420 – 5	1	3-wood		★		★			Unhappy
	2	7-iron		★			★		Happy
	3	5-iron		★				★	Happy
	4	SW			★			★	Unhappy
	5	putter		★			★		Happy
10 par 3 182 – 11	1	5-iron	★			★			Unhappy
	2	SW			★		★		Unhappy
	3	putter	★			★			Unhappy
	4	putter		★			★		Happy
11 par 4 363 – 6	1	3-wood			★	★			Unhappy
	2	2-iron			★	★			Unhappy
	3	7-iron		★			★		Happy
	4	putter		★				★	Unhappy
	5	putter		★			★		Happy

Key Holes show as:	Clubs: SW = Sand Wedge, PW = Pitching Wedge.
No. 1 par 4 yards 264 index 18	Shots: Length: L–Long; M–Medium; Sh–Short Position: L–Left; C–Centre, R–Right (of target aimed at, not pin)

Hole	Shot	Club	Length			Position			Happy/Unhappy
			L	M	S	L	C	R	
12 par 4 426 – 1	1	3-wood		★				★	Unhappy
	2	5-iron		★			★		Happy
	3	9-iron			★			★	Unhappy
	4	PW			★		★		Unhappy
	5	putter			★			★	Unhappy
	6	putter		★			★		Happy
13 par 4 314 – 15	1	3-wood	★			★			Happy
	2	8-iron		★				★	Happy
	3	putter			★			★	Happy
	4	putter		★			★		Happy
14 par 4 399 – 8	1	3-wood		★		★			Happy
	2	7-iron			★		★		Unhappy
	3	putter			★		★		Unhappy
	4	putter		★			★		Happy
15 par 3 139 – 17	1	5-iron		★				★	Unhappy
	2	SW		★				★	Unhappy
	3	putter	☆					★	Unhappy
	4	putter		★			★		Happy
16 par 4 416 – 4	1	3-wood	★				★		Happy
	2	4-iron		★			★		Happy
	3	PW			★		★		Unhappy
	4	putter							Unhappy
	5	putter		★			★		Happy
17 par 5 486 – 13	1	1-wood		★			★		Happy
	2	4-iron		★				★	Happy
	3	9-iron		★				★	Unhappy
	4	SW	★				★		Unhappy
	5	putter	★			★			Unhappy
	6	putter		★			★		Happy
18 par 4 417 – 10	1	3-wood		★		★			Unhappy
	2	6-iron	★					★	Happy
	3	9-iron			★		★		Unhappy
	4	putter		★				★	Happy
	5	putter		★			★		Happy

93

Net result:

1. Bogey	10. Par
2. Par	11. Par
3. Par	12. Bogey
4. Birdie	13. Par
5. Par	14. Birdie
6. Par	15. Bogey
7. Par	16. Par
8. Par	17. Par
9. Par	18. Par

Par – 13; Birdie – 2; Bogey – 3.

Player's handicap: 14.

Total score: 84, less 14, net 70. Course plays 69.

Analysis:

Tee shots were generally reasonable length, using primarily a 3-wood, which is sensible for this handicap. A driver would give no substantial benefit and the 3-wood feels more comfortable. Many tee-shots fell a little left, yet approach shots were mainly right and short, a fault of most middle and higher handicap players. By using too little club the shot was forced and pushed right. Either the club-face was open at contact or alignment is wrong. If open the club selection could be correct but the fade induced causes the ball to travel less.

A solution could be to try to hook the ball on approach shots slightly, provided the approach to the green is safe from the right hand side. This will make the ball run to the hole. Alternatively, use more club and hit the ball higher to land closer to, or just past, the pin. Too many players land short!

Putting appears satisfactory (34 for the round), though the player felt unhappy about it. (He was using a new putter this day!) Only one bunker shot – out first time but slightly short of the pin. Sand was wet.

The *net* result looks fairly satisfactory, though the player's comments demonstrated that he felt he could have shaved about six shots off this total with better approaches and a little more care. This proves how easy it is to knock a few strokes off a middle/high handicap. Six shots off this total would have given a gross score of just 78 – good enough to reduce a handicap to 9 – the magic single figure handicap!

Notes

Distances hit (average of 6 balls)

Weather cold and damp (add up to 20 yards on longer shots in hot weather). Sea-level. No wind. Ball always in good lie on short grass. Hit straight, without fade or draw (add five per cent for draw; subtract ten per cent for fade).

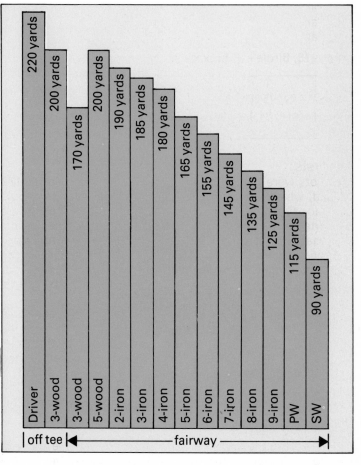

Driver	220 yards
3-wood	200 yards
3-wood	170 yards
5-wood	200 yards
2-iron	190 yards
3-iron	185 yards
4-iron	180 yards
5-iron	165 yards
6-iron	155 yards
7-iron	145 yards
8-iron	135 yards
9-iron	125 yards
PW	115 yards
SW	90 yards

off tee |← —————— fairway —————— →|

These are distances using graphite-shaft clubs (metal woods, also graphite shafts).

The problem which average players have with long irons is evident. The increase in yardage is only 5 yards between 4–3–2, whereas it is 10–15 yards with medium and short irons.

And finally . . .

Now that you have read this book and learnt how to conquer hazards, or how to avoid them altogether, I would like to pass on to you another secret of how to *really* improve your golf.

Practice, of course, makes perfect – or perhaps better than before – yet not everyone has the time, opportunity, facilities or even the desire to practise. Even I do not get as much time to practise, or play, as I would like.

To practise well, or at least to gain some benefit from an hour on the practice tee, you must have some goal in mind before you start. There may be a particular aspect of your game that you wish to improve. If so, you already have a motive to practise, whether it be your driving, chipping, bunker play, middle irons, short irons, long irons or, what for most people is fifty per cent of their game, putting.

Some countries, or clubs, do not have proper practice facilities – in Britain during the winter I, like others, have only floodlit driving ranges to use during the week. Rubber mats are no place to practise anything but tee shots; however, you have to make the most of what is available.

When faced with an evening at the driving range and having warmed up with a dozen 7-irons, I play a 'round', using any course I know well as my model.

I begin with a drive, trying to visualize where I want the ball to go, and imagining how far I have for the second shot, which might, for example, be a 5-iron. I then hit that to my 'green' – sometimes missing my aiming point on the range and practising a short pitch. It is impossible to play a chip or to putt, of course.

I then move on to the 2nd hole, which might be a short par-3 in which case I tee up a 5-wood, or 7-iron or whatever, and repeat the process until I have played nine holes. It livens up the practice session, although I get some strange looks sometimes from my fellow golfers.

Of course, if there is one part of my game with which I am unhappy, I will spend time working on that, experimenting on the range rather than on the course. When on the course I do not want to be tinkering with grip, swing or anything other than strategy.